**U.S. Department of Justice**
Office of Justice Programs
*Office of Juvenile Justice and Delinquency Prevention*

I0450387

*Juvenile Offenders and Victims:*

# National Report Series

*Bulletin*

December 2013

*This bulletin is part of the Juvenile Offenders and Victims National Report Series. The* National Report *offers a comprehensive statistical overview of the problems of juvenile crime, violence, and victimization and the response of the juvenile justice system. During each interim year, the bulletins in the* National Report Series *provide access to the latest information on juvenile arrests, court cases, juveniles in custody, and other topics of interest. Each bulletin in the series highlights selected topics at the forefront of juvenile justice policymaking, giving readers focused access to statistics on some of the most critical issues. Together, the* National Report *and this series provide a baseline of facts for juvenile justice professionals, policymakers, the media, and concerned citizens.*

# Juvenile Arrests 2010

Charles Puzzanchera

## A Message From OJJDP

This bulletin uses data from the Federal Bureau of Investigation's Uniform Crime Reporting program to summarize juvenile crime in the United States. Overall, in 2010, juveniles were arrested about 21% less often than in 2001. In fact, the number of juveniles arrested for violent crimes was at its lowest in at least 30 years, showing a 12% reduction between 2009 and 2010 and continuing a 4-year decline. The rate for overall juvenile arrests also fell 9% between 2009 and 2010.

A comparison of juveniles with adults in 2010 indicates that juveniles made up a relatively small proportion of all arrests—about 1 in 10 arrests for murder; about 1 in 4 for robbery, burglary, and disorderly conduct; and about 1 in 5 arrests for larceny-theft and motor vehicle theft. Even when arrest rates rose for juvenile offending, the rates were still low when compared with rates in the late 1990s and early 2000s.

As in past years, however, youth who are members of minority groups were overrepresented in the arrest data, calling for continued work to alleviate their disproportionate contact with the juvenile justice system. For example, the racial disparity in juvenile arrest rates for robbery was most pronounced for black youth, who were arrested at 10 times the rate for white youth in 2010.

OJJDP remains committed to supporting research, programs, and initiatives to combat juvenile delinquency and to promote positive youth outcomes. Should our children come into contact with the juvenile justice system, however, the contact should be rare, fair, and beneficial to them.

Robert L. Listenbee
Administrator

# Most information about law enforcement's response to juvenile crime comes from the FBI's UCR Program

## Since the 1930s, police agencies have reported to the UCR Program

Each year, thousands of police agencies voluntarily report the following data to the Federal Bureau of Investigation's (FBI's) Uniform Crime Reporting (UCR) Program:

■ Number of Index crimes reported to law enforcement (see sidebar).

■ Number of arrests and the most serious charge involved in each arrest.

■ Age, sex, and race of arrestees.

■ Proportion of reported Index crimes cleared by arrest and the proportion of these Index crimes cleared by the arrest of persons younger than 18.

■ Police dispositions of juvenile arrests.

■ Detailed victim, assailant, and circumstance information in murder cases.

## What can the UCR arrest data tell us about crime and young people?

The UCR arrest data can provide estimates of the annual number of arrests of juveniles* within specific offense categories. UCR data can also provide detail on juvenile arrests by sex, race, and type of location (urban, suburban, or rural area). The data can be used to compare the relative number of arrests of adults and juveniles within offense categories, to develop estimates of change in arrests over various periods, and to monitor the proportion of crimes cleared by arrests of juveniles.

---

* In this bulletin, the term "juvenile" refers to persons younger than age 18. In 2010, this definition was at odds with the legal definition of juveniles in 13 states—11 states where all 17-year-olds are defined as adults, and 2 states where all 16- and 17-year-olds are defined as adults.

## What do arrest statistics count?

To interpret the material in this bulletin properly, the reader needs a clear understanding of what these statistics count. Arrest statistics report the number of arrests that law enforcement agencies made in a given year—not the number of individuals arrested nor the number of crimes committed. The number of arrests is not the same as the number of people arrested because an unknown number of individuals are arrested more than once during the year. Nor do arrest statistics represent the number of crimes that arrested individuals commit because a series of crimes that one person commits may culminate in a single arrest, and a single crime may result in the arrest of more than one person. This latter situation, where many arrests result from one crime, is relatively common in juvenile law-violating behavior because juveniles are more likely than adults to commit crimes in groups. For this reason, one should not use arrest statistics to indicate the relative proportions of crime that juveniles and adults commit. Arrest statistics are most appropriately a measure of entry into the justice system.

Arrest statistics also have limitations in measuring the volume of arrests for a particular offense. Under the UCR Program, the FBI requires law enforcement agencies to classify an arrest by the most serious offense charged in that arrest. For example, the arrest of a youth charged with aggravated assault and possession of a weapon would be reported to the FBI as an arrest for aggravated assault. Therefore, when arrest statistics show that law enforcement agencies made an estimated 31,400 arrests of young people for weapons law violations in 2010, it means that a weapons law violation was

the most serious charge in these 31,400 arrests. An unknown number of additional arrests in 2010 included a weapons charge as a lesser offense.

---

## What are the Crime Indexes?

The designers of the UCR Program wanted to create an index (similar in concept to the Dow Jones Industrial Average or the Consumer Price Index) that would be sensitive to changes in the volume and nature of reported crime. They decided to incorporate specific offenses into the index, based on several factors: likelihood of being reported, frequency of occurrence, pervasiveness in all geographical areas of the country, and relative seriousness.

The Crime Index is divided into two components: the Violent Crime Index and the Property Crime Index.

**Violent Crime Index**—Includes murder and nonnegligent manslaughter, forcible rape, robbery, and aggravated assault.

**Property Crime Index**—Includes burglary, larceny-theft, motor vehicle theft, and arson.

Although some violent crimes, such as kidnapping and extortion, are excluded, the Violent Crime Index contains what are generally considered to be serious crimes. In contrast, a substantial proportion of the crimes in the Property Crime Index are generally considered to be less serious crimes, such as shoplifting, theft from motor vehicles, and bicycle theft, all of which are included in the larceny-theft category.

---

## What do clearance statistics count?

Clearance statistics measure the proportion of reported crimes that were cleared (or "closed") by either arrest or other, exceptional means (such as the death of the offender or unwillingness of the victim to cooperate). A single arrest may result in many clearances. For example, 1 arrest could clear 10 burglaries if the person was charged with committing all 10 crimes. Or multiple arrests may result in a single clearance if a group of offenders committed the crime. For those interested in juvenile justice issues, the FBI also reports the proportion of clearances that involved only offenders younger than age 18. This statistic is a better indicator of the proportion of crime that this age group commits than is the proportion of arrests, although there are some concerns that even the clearance statistic overestimates the proportion of crimes that juveniles commit.

| Most serious offense | Percent involving juveniles | |
|---|---|---|
| | Clearance | Arrest |
| Violent Crime Index | 10% | 14% |
| Property Crime Index | 16 | 22 |
| Murder | 5 | 9 |
| Forcible rape | 11 | 14 |
| Robbery | 14 | 24 |
| Aggravated assault | 9 | 11 |
| Burglary | 14 | 23 |
| Larceny-theft | 17 | 22 |
| Motor vehicle theft | 13 | 22 |
| Arson | 34 | 40 |

**Data source:** *Crime in the United States 2010* (Washington, DC: Federal Bureau of Investigation, 2011), tables 28 and 38.

Research has shown that juvenile offenders are more easily apprehended than adult offenders; thus, the juvenile proportion of clearances probably overestimates juveniles' responsibility for crime. To add to the difficulty in interpreting clearance statistics, the FBI's reporting guidelines require that clearances involving both juvenile and adult offenders be classified as clearances for crimes that adults commit. Because the juvenile clearance proportions include only those clearances in which no adults were involved, they underestimate juvenile involvement in crime. Although these data do not present a definitive picture of juvenile involvement in crime, they are the closest measure generally available of the proportion of crime known to law enforcement that is attributed to persons younger than age 18.

## How are national estimates of arrests calculated?

The FBI's *Crime in the United States* (*CIUS*) report presents a detailed snapshot of crime and arrests voluntarily reported by local law enforcement agencies. Some agencies report data for a full calendar year, other agencies are "partial reporters" (i.e., their reported data cover less than 12 months), and some agencies do not report at all. Data from 12-month reporting agencies form the basis of the tables presented in the annual *CIUS* report. As such, *CIUS* presents a sample-based portrait of arrests that law enforcement agencies report. Although the *CIUS* report includes one table that presents national estimates of arrests for 29 offense categories for the current data year, it does not include national estimates for any subpopulation groups.

For nearly two decades, the National Center for Juvenile Justice developed national estimates of juvenile arrests based on data presented in *CIUS*; these estimates have been the basis of the *Juvenile Arrests* series since its inception in the 1990s. In 2009, however, the Bureau of Justice Statistics (BJS) developed a new process that supplants the estimation procedure used in prior versions of this bulletin. The method that BJS uses takes advantage of more complete sample data reported to the FBI from local law enforcement agencies. To learn more about the BJS estimation process, see *Arrest in the United States, 1980–2010*, which is available from the BJS Web site (bjs.gov).

### *Crime in the United States* reports data on murder victims

Each *Crime in the United States* report presents estimates of the number of crimes reported to law enforcement agencies. Although many crimes are never reported to law enforcement, murder is one crime that is nearly always reported.

An estimated 14,750 murders were reported to law enforcement agencies in 2010, or 4.8 murders for every 100,000 U.S. residents. The murder rate was essentially constant between 1999 and 2008, and then fell in 2010 to its lowest level since at least 1980.

Of all murder victims in 2010, 90% (or 13,280 victims) were 18 years old or older. The other 1,470 murder victims were younger than age 18 (i.e., juveniles). The number of juveniles murdered in 2010 was 14% less than the average number of juveniles murdered in the prior 5-year period and 49% less than the peak year of 1993, when an estimated 2,880 juveniles were murdered. During the same prior 5-year period, the estimated number of adult murder victims fell 10%.

Of all juveniles murdered in 2010, 39% were younger than age 5, 70% were male, and 48% were white. Of all juveniles murdered in 2010, 32% of male victims, 56% of female victims, 50% of white victims, and 29% of black victims were younger than age 5.

In 2010, 68% of all murder victims were killed with a firearm. Adults were more likely to be killed with a firearm (70%) than were juveniles (49%). However, the involvement of a firearm depended greatly on the age of the juvenile victim. In 2010, 15% of murdered juveniles younger than age 13 were killed with a firearm, compared with 82% of murdered juveniles age 13 or older. The most common method of murdering children younger than age 5 was by physical assault: in 46% of these murders, the offenders' only weapons were their hands and/or feet, compared with only 1% of juvenile victims age 13 or older and 4% of adult victims.

# Law enforcement agencies in the U.S. made 1.6 million arrests of persons under age 18 in 2010

**The number of arrests of juveniles in 2010 was 21% fewer than the number of arrests in 2001**

| Most serious offense | 2010 estimated number of juvenile arrests | Percent of total juvenile arrests | | | Percent change | | |
|---|---|---|---|---|---|---|---|
| | | Female | Younger than 15 | White | 2001–2010 | 2006–2010 | 2009–2010 |
| **Total** | 1,642,600 | 29% | 27% | 66% | −21% | −22% | −9% |
| **Violent Crime Index** | 75,900 | 18 | 27 | 47 | −22 | −24 | −12 |
| Murder and nonnegligent manslaughter | 1,000 | 10 | 9 | 43 | −20 | −21 | −14 |
| Forcible rape | 2,900 | 2 | 33 | 63 | −37 | −20 | −8 |
| Robbery | 27,200 | 10 | 19 | 31 | 3 | −22 | −14 |
| Aggravated assault | 44,800 | 25 | 31 | 56 | −31 | −26 | −10 |
| **Property Crime Index** | 366,600 | 38 | 28 | 64 | −25 | −9 | −12 |
| Burglary | 65,200 | 11 | 27 | 62 | −27 | −22 | −13 |
| Larceny-theft | 281,100 | 45 | 28 | 65 | −18 | 2 | −12 |
| Motor vehicle theft | 15,800 | 16 | 20 | 55 | −67 | −54 | −21 |
| Arson | 4,600 | 13 | 58 | 75 | −52 | −44 | −15 |
| **Nonindex** | | | | | | | |
| Other (simple) assaults | 210,200 | 35 | 38 | 60 | −13 | −16 | −4 |
| Forgery and counterfeiting | 1,700 | 27 | 12 | 67 | −71 | −52 | −21 |
| Fraud | 5,800 | 34 | 16 | 59 | −58 | −23 | −6 |
| Embezzlement | 400 | 41 | 5 | 63 | −77 | −68 | −27 |
| Stolen property (buying, receiving, possessing) | 14,600 | 16 | 22 | 56 | −43 | −31 | −22 |
| Vandalism | 77,100 | 15 | 39 | 78 | −27 | −34 | −15 |
| Weapons (carrying, possessing, etc.) | 31,400 | 11 | 33 | 62 | −15 | −33 | −7 |
| Prostitution and commercialized vice | 1,000 | 82 | 11 | 38 | −29 | −33 | −23 |
| Sex offense (except forcible rape and prostitution) | 13,000 | 10 | 48 | 72 | −30 | −19 | −4 |
| Drug abuse violations | 170,600 | 16 | 18 | 74 | −15 | −13 | 0 |
| Gambling | 1,400 | 3 | 11 | 8 | 31 | −37 | −24 |
| Offenses against the family and children | 3,800 | 35 | 32 | 72 | −58 | −30 | −15 |
| Driving under the influence | 12,000 | 25 | 2 | 91 | −42 | −40 | −11 |
| Liquor laws | 94,700 | 39 | 10 | 88 | −13 | −32 | −14 |
| Drunkenness | 12,700 | 27 | 12 | 89 | −38 | −22 | −8 |
| Disorderly conduct | 155,900 | 34 | 37 | 58 | −6 | −25 | −8 |
| Vagrancy | 2,100 | 23 | 28 | 76 | −22 | −57 | −22 |
| All other offenses (except traffic) | 296,800 | 26 | 23 | 69 | −22 | −23 | −8 |
| Suspicion (not included in totals) | 100 | 23 | 26 | 68 | −89 | −70 | −40 |
| Curfew and loitering | 94,800 | 30 | 25 | 59 | −34 | −38 | −16 |

- In 2010, there were an estimated 170,600 juvenile arrests for drug abuse violations. Between 2001 and 2010, the number of such arrests fell by 15%.

- All four offenses that make up the Violent Crime Index decreased between 2009 and 2010: murder (down 14%), rape (8%), robbery (14%), and aggravated assault (10%).

- In 2010, females accounted for 18% of juvenile Violent Crime Index arrests, 38% of juvenile Property Crime Index arrests, and 45% of juvenile larceny-theft arrests.

- Youth younger than age 15 accounted for more than one-fourth of all juvenile arrests for Violent Crime Index offenses and Property Crime Index offenses in 2010 (27% and 28%, respectively).

**Note:** Detail may not add to totals because of rounding. The FBI stopped reporting runaway offenses as of 2010.

**Data source:** Analysis of Snyder, H., and Mulako-Wantota, J., Bureau of Justice Statistics, *Arrest Data Analysis Tool* [online, retrieved 11/8/12].

# The number of juvenile Violent Crime Index offense arrests in 2010 was the lowest since at least 1980

## Juvenile arrests for violence declined in 2010 for the fourth consecutive year

The FBI assesses trends in violent crimes by monitoring four offenses that law enforcement agencies nationwide consistently report. These four crimes—murder and nonnegligent manslaughter, forcible rape, robbery, and aggravated assault—form the Violent Crime Index.

Following 10 years of declines between 1994 and 2004, juvenile arrests for Violent Crime Index offenses increased from 2004 to 2006, then declined in each of the next 4 years. In fact, the number of juvenile violent crime arrests in 2010 was less than any of the prior 30 years, and 6% less than the previous low point in 1984.

The number of juvenile arrests in 2010 for forcible rape was less than in any year since at least 1980, and the number of juvenile aggravated assault arrests in 2010 was at the lowest level in over 20 years. After falling to a relatively low level in 2004, juvenile arrests for murder increased each year from 2005 to 2007, then declined 24% by 2010 to reach the lowest level in 3 decades. However, juvenile arrests for robbery increased 43% from 2002 through 2009, then declined 21% by 2010, resulting in a rate 11% above the 2002 low point.

Between 2001 and 2010, the number of arrests in most offense categories declined for juveniles but increased in several offense categories for adults:

| Most serious offense | Percent change in arrests 2001–2010 | |
|---|---|---|
| | Juvenile | Adult |
| Violent Crime Index | −22% | −10% |
| Murder | −20 | −18 |
| Forcible rape | −37 | −24 |
| Robbery | 3 | 4 |
| Aggravated assault | −31 | −12 |
| Property Crime Index | −25 | 13 |
| Burglary | −27 | 11 |
| Larceny-theft | −18 | 21 |
| Motor vehicle theft | −67 | −44 |
| Simple assault | −13 | 1 |
| Weapons law violations | −15 | −1 |
| Drug abuse violations | −15 | 6 |

**Data source:** Analysis of Snyder, H., and Mulako-Wantota, J., Bureau of Justice Statistics, *Arrest Data Analysis Tool* [online, retrieved 11/8/12].

## Juvenile property crime arrests declined in 2010

As with violent crime, the FBI assesses trends in the volume of property crimes by monitoring four offenses that law enforcement agencies nationwide consistently report. These four crimes, which form the Property Crime Index, are burglary, larceny-theft, motor vehicle theft, and arson.

For the period 1980–1994, during which juvenile violent crime arrests increased substantially, juvenile property crime arrests remained relatively constant. After this long period of relative stability, juvenile property crime arrests began to fall. Between 1994 and 2006, the number of juvenile Property Crime Index arrests fell by half to their lowest level since at least 1980. This long decline was interrupted briefly as the number of juvenile Property Crime Index arrests increased in 2007 and 2008. By 2010, the number of juvenile Property Crime Index arrests fell 16%, reaching its lowest level since at least 1980. Between 2008 and 2010, juvenile arrests declined for individual property offenses: burglary (22%), larceny-theft (13%), motor vehicle theft (37%), and arson (30%). Juvenile arrests for burglary, motor vehicle theft, and arson in 2010 were at their lowest levels for the 31-year period.

---

### Most arrested juveniles were referred to court

In most states, some persons younger than age 18 are, because of their age or by statutory exclusion, under the jurisdiction of the criminal justice system. For arrested persons younger than age 18 and under the original jurisdiction of their state's juvenile justice system, the FBI's UCR Program monitors what happens as a result of the arrest. This is the only instance in the UCR Program in which the statistics on arrests coincide with state variations in the legal definition of a juvenile.

In 2010, 23% of arrests involving youth who were eligible in their state for processing in the juvenile justice system were handled within law enforcement agencies and the youth were released, 68% were referred to juvenile court, and 8% were referred directly to criminal court. The others were referred to a welfare agency or to another police agency. The proportion of juvenile arrests sent to juvenile court in cities with a population of more than 250,000 was less than the proportion sent to juvenile court in smaller cities (64% vs. 68%).

**Data source:** *Crime in the United States 2010* (Washington, DC: Federal Bureau of Investigation, 2011), table 68.

---

# Female and minority proportions of juvenile arrests increased for many offenses between 2001 and 2010

## In 2010, females accounted for 29% of juvenile arrests

Law enforcement agencies made 480,000 arrests of females younger than age 18 in 2010. From 2001 through 2010, arrests of juvenile females decreased less than male arrests in several offense categories (e.g., aggravated assault, simple assault, larceny-theft, vandalism, drug abuse violations, and driving under the influence).

| Most serious offense | Percent change in juvenile arrests 2001–2010 | |
|---|---|---|
| | Female | Male |
| Violent Crime Index | −22% | −22% |
| Robbery | 13 | 2 |
| Aggravated assault | −27 | −33 |
| Simple assault | −3 | −17 |
| Property Crime Index | −9 | −32 |
| Burglary | −29 | −27 |
| Larceny-theft | −4 | −27 |
| Motor vehicle theft | −69 | −67 |
| Vandalism | −17 | −28 |
| Weapons | −17 | −15 |
| Drug abuse violations | −9 | −16 |
| Liquor law violations | 6 | −21 |
| Driving under influence | −19 | −47 |
| Disorderly conduct | 10 | −12 |

**Data source:** Analysis of Snyder, H., and Mulako-Wantota, J., Bureau of Justice Statistics, *Arrest Data Analysis Tool* [online, retrieved 11/8/12].

Gender differences also occurred in the assault arrest trends for adults. Between 2001 and 2010, adult male arrests for aggravated assault fell 15% while female arrests were virtually unchanged. Similarly, adult male arrests for simple assault fell 4% between 2001 and 2010 while adult female arrests rose 18%. Therefore, the female proportion of arrests grew for both types of assault. It is likely that the disproportionate growth in female assault arrests over this period was related to factors that affected both juveniles and adults.

Gender differences in arrest trends also increased the proportion of arrests involving females in other offense categories for both juveniles and adults. Between 2001 and 2010, the number of larceny-theft arrests of juvenile females fell 4% while juvenile male arrests declined 27%, and adult female arrests grew more than adult male arrests (47% and 7%, respectively). For Property Crime Index offenses, juvenile arrests declined more for males than for females between 2001 and 2010, and adult arrests increased less for males (1%) than for females (42%).

## Juvenile arrests disproportionately involved minorities

The racial composition of the U.S. juvenile population ages 10–17 in 2010 was 76% white, 17% black, 5% Asian/Pacific Islander, and 1% American Indian. Most juveniles of Hispanic ethnicity were included in the white racial category. Of all juvenile arrests for violent crimes in 2010, 47% involved white youth, 51% involved black youth, 1% involved Asian youth, and 1% involved American Indian youth. For property crime arrests, the proportions were 64% white youth, 33% black youth, 2% Asian youth, and 1% American Indian youth. Black youth were overrepresented in juvenile arrests.

| Most serious offense | Black proportion of juvenile arrests in 2010 |
|---|---|
| Murder | 56% |
| Forcible rape | 36 |
| Robbery | 67 |
| Aggravated assault | 41 |
| Simple assault | 38 |
| Burglary | 36 |
| Larceny-theft | 32 |
| Motor vehicle theft | 42 |
| Weapons | 36 |
| Drug abuse violations | 24 |
| Vandalism | 20 |
| Liquor laws | 7 |

**Data source:** Analysis of Snyder, H., and Mulako-Wantota, J., Bureau of Justice Statistics, *Arrest Data Analysis Tool* [online, retrieved 11/8/12].

### One in nine violent crimes cleared was attributed to juveniles

The relative responsibility of juveniles and adults for crime is difficult to determine. Law enforcement agencies are more likely to clear (or "close") crimes that juveniles commit than those that adults commit. Thus, law enforcement records may overestimate juvenile responsibility for crime.

Data on crimes cleared or closed by arrest or exceptional means show that the proportion of violent crimes cleared and attributed to juveniles has been rather constant in recent years, holding at about 12% over the past 10 years. Specifically, the proportions of both forcible rapes and aggravated assaults attributed to juveniles fluctuated between 10% and 12% over this period, while the proportion of murders ranged between 5% and 6% and the proportion of robberies ranged between 14% and 16%.

In 2010, 16% of Property Crime Index offenses cleared by arrest or exceptional means were cleared by the arrest of a juvenile. This was the lowest level since at least the mid-1960s. For comparison, the proportion of Property Crime Index offenses that law enforcement attributed to juveniles was 28% in 1980 and 22% in both 1990 and 2001.

**In 2010, juveniles were involved in about 1 in 10 arrests for murder; about 1 in 4 arrests for robbery, burglary, and disorderly conduct; and about 1 in 5 arrests for larceny-theft and motor vehicle theft**

| Most serious offense | Juvenile arrests as a percentage of total arrests | | | | | | |
|---|---|---|---|---|---|---|---|
| | All persons | Males | Females | Whites | Blacks | American Indians | Asians |
| Total | 12% | 11% | 14% | 11% | 13% | 10% | 14% |
| **Violent Crime Index** | 14 | 14 | 13 | 11 | 18 | 9 | 12 |
| Murder and nonnegligent manslaughter | 9 | 9 | 8 | 8 | 10 | 4 | 7 |
| Forcible rape | 14 | 14 | 29 | 14 | 16 | 9 | 7 |
| Robbery | 24 | 25 | 19 | 18 | 29 | 16 | 26 |
| Aggravated assault | 11 | 11 | 12 | 10 | 14 | 9 | 9 |
| **Property Crime Index** | 22 | 22 | 23 | 21 | 26 | 21 | 29 |
| Burglary | 23 | 23 | 17 | 21 | 27 | 21 | 26 |
| Larceny-theft | 22 | 21 | 23 | 21 | 25 | 20 | 30 |
| Motor vehicle theft | 22 | 22 | 20 | 19 | 28 | 25 | 20 |
| Arson | 40 | 42 | 31 | 40 | 40 | 40 | 52 |
| **Nonindex** | | | | | | | |
| Other assaults | 16 | 14 | 21 | 15 | 20 | 11 | 15 |
| Forgery and counterfeiting | 2 | 3 | 2 | 2 | 2 | 2 | 3 |
| Fraud | 3 | 3 | 2 | 3 | 4 | 4 | 4 |
| Embezzlement | 3 | 3 | 2 | 3 | 3 | 4 | 3 |
| Stolen property (buying, receiving, possessing) | 15 | 16 | 13 | 13 | 20 | 14 | 17 |
| Vandalism | 30 | 32 | 24 | 32 | 26 | 23 | 31 |
| Weapons (carrying, possessing, etc.) | 20 | 19 | 25 | 21 | 18 | 21 | 25 |
| Prostitution and commercialized vice | 2 | 1 | 2 | 1 | 2 | 3 | 1 |
| Sex offense (except forcible rape and prostitution) | 18 | 17 | 23 | 17 | 20 | 10 | 18 |
| Drug abuse violations | 10 | 11 | 9 | 12 | 8 | 16 | 14 |
| Gambling | 14 | 15 | 5 | 4 | 18 | 10 | 3 |
| Offenses against the family and children | 3 | 3 | 5 | 4 | 3 | 5 | 3 |
| Driving under the influence | 1 | 1 | 1 | 1 | 0 | 1 | 1 |
| Liquor laws | 18 | 16 | 25 | 20 | 11 | 17 | 19 |
| Drunkenness | 2 | 2 | 3 | 2 | 1 | 3 | 3 |
| Disorderly conduct | 25 | 23 | 31 | 23 | 30 | 15 | 24 |
| Vagrancy | 7 | 6 | 8 | 9 | 4 | 1 | 7 |
| All other offenses (except traffic) | 8 | 8 | 9 | 8 | 7 | 6 | 11 |
| Suspicion (not included in totals) | 11 | 11 | 11 | 12 | 10 | 0 | 14 |

■ Juvenile females accounted for more than one-fifth (21%) of all simple assault arrests involving females in 2010, while male juveniles accounted for 14% of all simple assault arrests involving males.

■ On average, juveniles accounted for 9% of all murder arrests during the 2000s, compared with 14% during the 1990s.

■ Overall, in 2010, 11% of white arrests and 13% of black arrests involved a person younger than age 18. However, for some offenses, juveniles were involved in a greater proportion of black arrests than white arrests (e.g., robbery, burglary, and disorderly conduct). For other offenses, juvenile involvement was greater in white arrests than black arrests (e.g., vandalism, and liquor law violations).

**Note:** Detail may not add to totals because of rounding.

**Data source:** Analysis of Snyder, H., and Mulako-Wantota, J., Bureau of Justice Statistics, *Arrest Data Analysis Tool* [online, retrieved 11/8/12].

# The juvenile Violent Crime Index arrest rate reached a historic low in 2010

## Violent crime arrest rates declined after 1994

Between 1980 and 1987, the juvenile Violent Crime Index arrest rate (i.e., the number of arrests per 100,000 juveniles in the population) was essentially constant. After these years of stability, the rate grew by nearly 70% in the 7-year period between 1987 and 1994. This rapid growth led to speculation about changes in the nature of juvenile offenders—concerns that spurred state legislators to pass laws that facilitated an increase in the flow of youth into the adult justice system. After 1994, however, the violent crime arrest rate fell. Between 1994 and 2010, the rate fell 55% to its lowest level since at least 1980.

## Female violent crime arrest rates remain relatively high

In 1980, the juvenile male violent crime arrest rate was 8 times greater than the female rate. By 2010, the male rate was just 4 times greater. This convergence of male and female arrest rates is due to the large relative increase in the female rate. Between 1980 and 1994, the male rate increased 60%, while the female rate increased 132%. By 2010, the male rate had dropped to 31% below its 1980 level, while the female violent crime arrest rate was still 36% above its 1980 level.

## Arrest rates declined for all racial groups since the mid-1990s

All racial groups experienced large increases in their juvenile violent crime arrest rates in the late 1980s and early 1990s. Following their mid-1990s peak,

**Following a 23% decline since 2006, the 2010 Violent Crime Index arrest rate reached its lowest level since at least 1980**

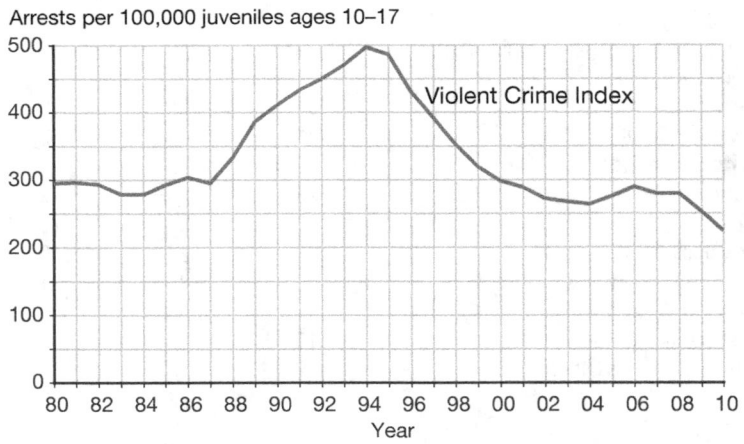

Arrests per 100,000 juveniles ages 10–17

**Violent Crime Index arrest rate trends by gender and race**

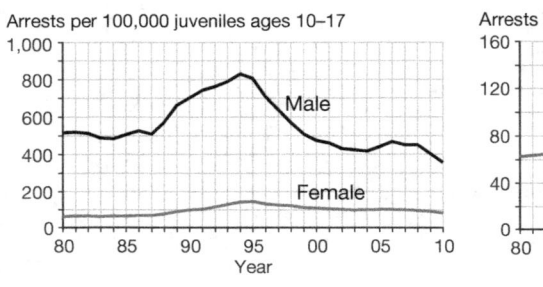

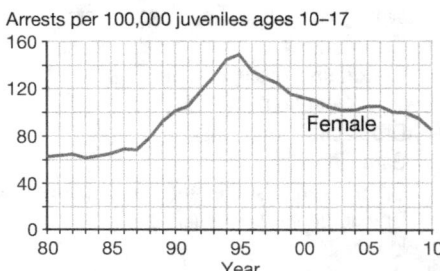

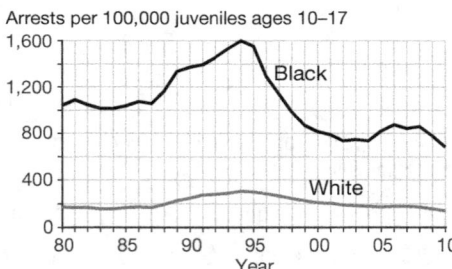

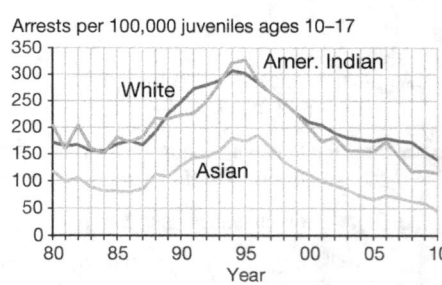

■ The Violent Crime Index arrest rate in 2010 for black juveniles was 5 times the rate for white juveniles, 6 times the rate for American Indian juveniles, and 15 times the rate for Asian juveniles.

**Data source:** Analysis of arrest data from the Bureau of Justice Statistics, and population data from the U.S. Bureau of the Census. (See arrest rate data source note on page 23 for details.)

the rates declined through 2010 for all racial groups: Asian (75%), American Indian (65%), black (57%), and white (54%) youth.

# The juvenile arrest rate for murder has remained relatively constant during the 2000s

## The 2010 murder arrest rate was the lowest since at least 1980

Between the mid-1980s and the peak in 1993, the juvenile arrest rate for murder more than doubled. Since the 1993 peak, however, the rate fell substantially through 2000, resting at a level that essentially remained constant for the entire decade. Compared with the prior 20 years, the juvenile murder arrest rate between 2000 and 2010 has been historically low and relatively stable. In fact, the number of juvenile arrests for murder in the 4-year period from 1992 through 1995 exceeded the total number of such arrests since 2000.

## Male arrests drove murder arrest rate trends

During the 1980s and 1990s, the juvenile male arrest rate for murder was, on average, about 13 times greater than the female rate. Both displayed generally similar trends. The female arrest rate peaked in 1994 at 62% above its 1980 level, whereas the male rate peaked in 1993 at 123% above the 1980 rate. Both fell more than 58% since their respective peaks so that, by 2010, both arrest rates were substantially below their levels of the early 1980s.

## The juvenile murder arrest rate pattern was linked to the arrests of black juveniles

The black-to-white ratio of juvenile arrest rates for murder grew from about 4-to-1 in 1980 to nearly 9-to-1 in 1993, reflecting the greater increase in the black rate over this period—the white rate increased 47% while the black rate tripled. Since the

**Following a 23% decline since 2007, the 2010 juvenile murder arrest rate was well below the levels reached during the 1990s**

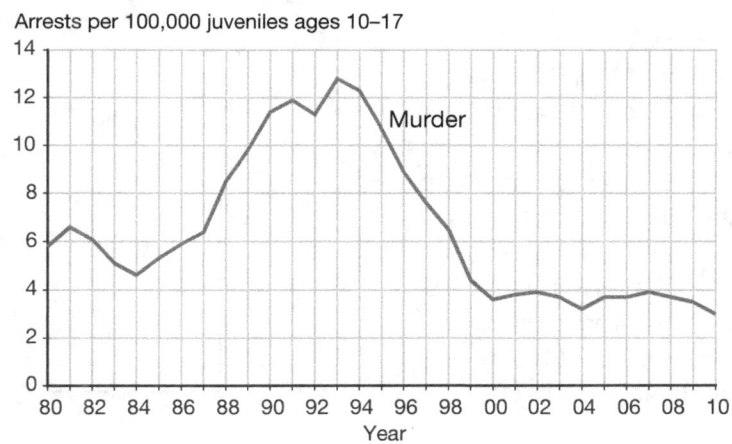

**Murder arrest rate trends by gender and race**

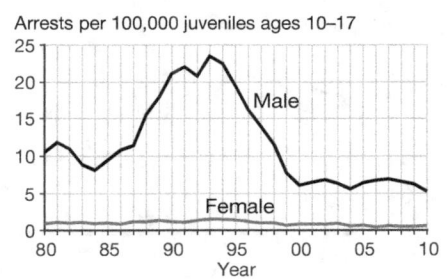

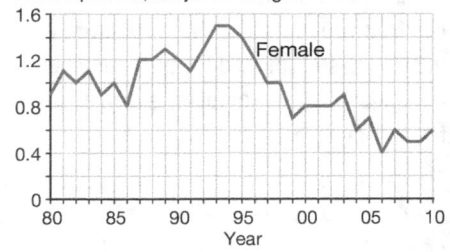

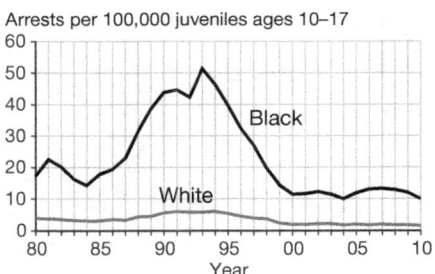

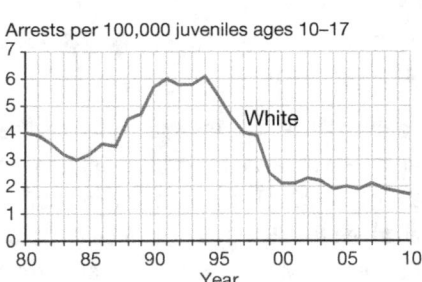

**Note**: Murder arrest rates for American Indian youth and Asian youth are not presented because the small number of arrests and small population sizes produce unstable rate trends.

**Data source**: Analysis of arrest data from the Bureau of Justice Statistics, and population data from the U.S. Bureau of the Census. (See arrest rate data source note on page 23 for details.)

1993 peak, both rates fell through 2000, with the black rate falling considerably more. During the past decade, the rates remained relatively constant. As a result, the black-to-white ratio of juvenile arrest rates for murder in 2010 approached 6-to-1.

# The juvenile arrest rate for forcible rape in 2010 was one third its 1991 peak

## The 2010 rape arrest rate was at its lowest level in three decades

Between 1980 and the peak in 1991, the juvenile arrest rate for forcible rape increased 50%. This growth occurred during a time when there were also increases in arrest rates for aggravated assault and murder. After 1991, the forcible rape arrest rate gradually fell, resting at a level in 2010 that was 62% below the 1991 peak. In fact, the 2,900 estimated juvenile arrests for forcible rape in 2010 were the fewest such arrests in at least three decades.

Juveniles accounted for 14% of all forcible rape arrests reported in 2010. Two-thirds (67%) of these juvenile arrests involved youth ages 15–17. Not surprisingly, males accounted for the overwhelming majority (98%) of juvenile arrests for forcible rape.

## Rape arrest rates declined more for black youth than white youth since 1991

For black juveniles, the substantial decline in the arrest rate for forcible rape began in the late 1980s. The rate peaked in 1987 and then fell 75% by 2010. In contrast to the rate for whites, the forcible rape arrest rate for black juveniles in 2010 was less than one-third the rate in 1980. For white juveniles, the arrest rate for forcible rape nearly doubled between 1980 and 1991, when it reached its peak. Between 1991 and 2010, the rate declined 55%, resting at its lowest level in at least 31 years. By 2010, the black-to-white ratio of juvenile arrest rates for forcible rape was less than 3-to-1, compared with a ratio of 7-to-1 in the early 1980s.

### With few exceptions, the juvenile arrest rate for forcible rape dropped annually from 1991 through 2010

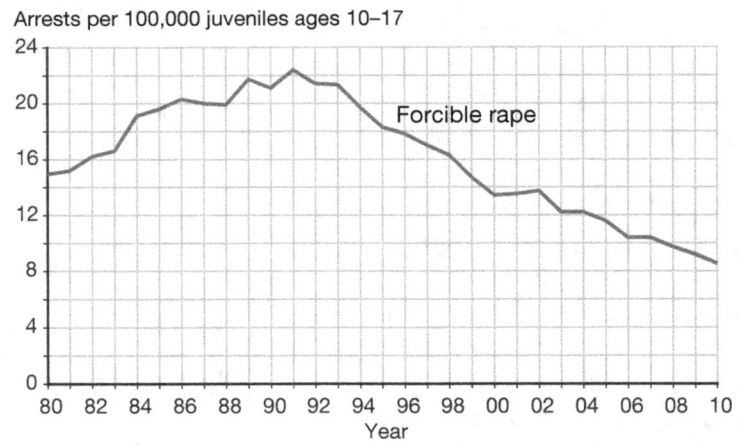

### Forcible rape arrest rate trends by gender and race

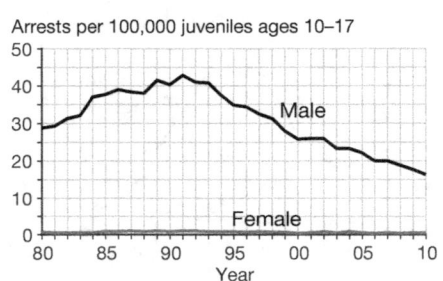
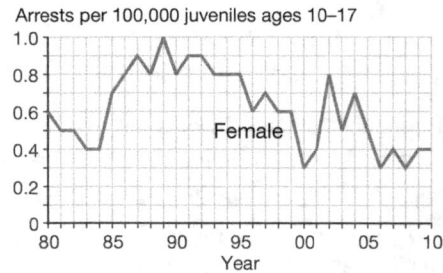
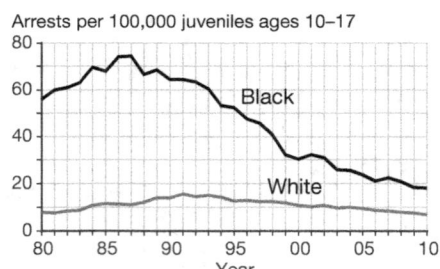
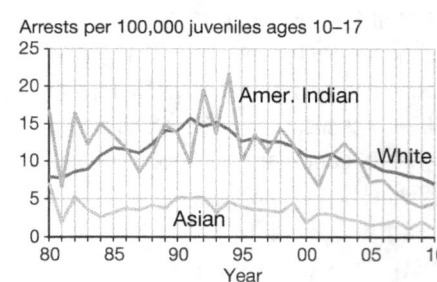

■ Black youth accounted for more than one-third (36%) of all juvenile arrests for forcible rape in 2010, and white youth accounted for nearly two-thirds (63%).

**Note:** The annual rape arrest rates for American Indians fluctuate because of the small number of arrests, but the average rate over the period is close to the white rate.

**Data source:** Analysis of arrest data from the Bureau of Justice Statistics, and population data from the U.S. Bureau of the Census. (See arrest rate data source note on page 23 for details.)

# The juvenile arrest rate for robbery declined substantially after its mid-1990s peak

## The juvenile arrest rate for robbery declined in the past 2 years

The juvenile arrest rate for robbery declined for most of the 1980s and then increased steadily to a peak in 1994. By 2002, the rate fell 60% from the 1994 peak and then increased yet again through 2008 (up 43%). Despite the decline since 2008 (down 22%), the rate in 2010 was 11% above its low point in 2002.

## Arrest rate trends by gender and race parallel the overall robbery arrest rate pattern

Across gender and race subgroups, robbery arrest rates decreased through the late 1980s and climbed to a peak in the mid-1990s. By 2002, the rate for males and females had fallen to their lowest level since at least 1980. Following these declines, the rates for both groups increased through 2008 (42% for males and 51% for females). Despite the decline over the previous 2 years, the rates for both groups in 2010 were above their 2002 low point.

The trends in arrest rates within racial groups were similar over the past three decades. For each racial group, the juvenile robbery arrest rate fell by more than 50% between the mid-1990s and the early 2000s. Juvenile robbery arrest rates increased for all but Asian youth since 2004. As a result, rates in 2010 were above the 2004 level for American Indian youth (21%), black youth (15%), and white youth (1%) and below the 2004 level for Asian youth (26%).

### The juvenile arrest rate for robbery reached a historically low level in 2002, 60% below the 1994 peak

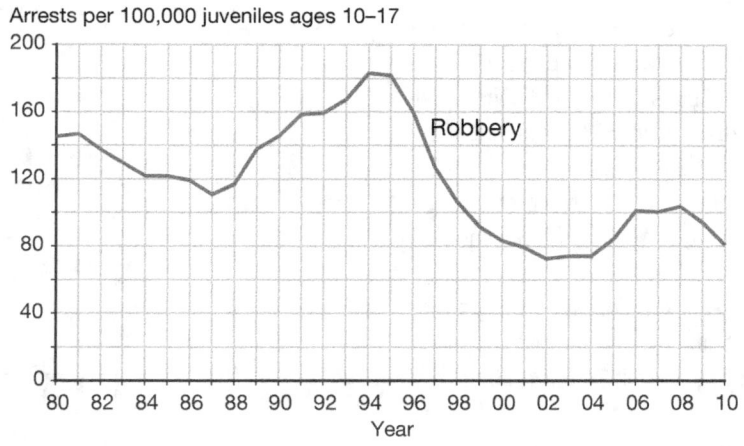

### Robbery arrest rate trends by gender and race

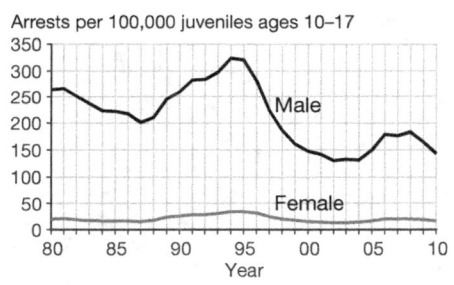
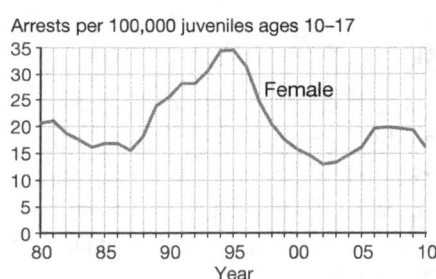
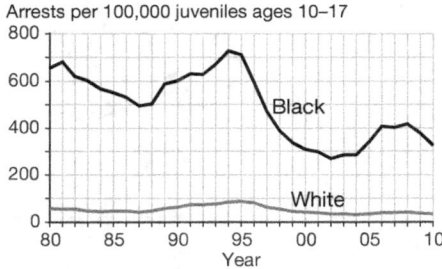
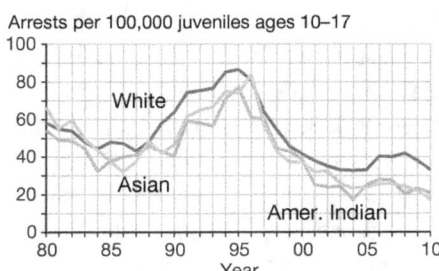

■ The racial disparity in juvenile arrest rates for robbery was quite large in 2010. Specifically, the rate for black youth was 10 times the rate for white youth, 15 times the rate for American Indian youth, and 19 times the rate for Asian youth.

**Data source:** Analysis of arrest data from the Bureau of Justice Statistics, and population data from the U.S. Bureau of the Census. (See arrest rate data source note on page 23 for details.)

# The 2010 juvenile arrest rate for aggravated assault was at its lowest since the early 1980s

## The juvenile aggravated assault arrest rate fell 53% since its 1994 peak

The juvenile arrest rate for aggravated assault doubled between 1980 and 1994 and then fell substantially and consistently through 2010, down 53% from its 1994 peak. As a result of this decline, the rate in 2010 returned to the level of the early 1980s, resting at a rate just 3% above the 1983 low point. However, of the four Violent Crime Index offenses, only aggravated assault had a juvenile arrest rate in 2010 above the levels of the 1980s.

## The rate for females increased more and declined less than the male rate

The juvenile arrest rate for aggravated assault doubled between 1980 and the mid-1990s for males, while the female rate increased by more than 170%. Since the mid-1990s peak, the rates for both groups declined through 2010, but the relative decline was greater for males (57%) than for females (40%). As a result, in 2010, the juvenile male arrest rate was 10% below its 1980 level, and the female rate was 68% above its 1980 level. The disproportionate increase in female arrest rates for aggravated assault compared with male rates indicates that factors that impinged differently on females and males affected the rates. One possible explanation may be found in policy changes over this period that encouraged arrests in domestic violence incidents.

## Aggravated assault arrest rates fell for all four racial groups

The period from 1980 through 1994 saw substantial increases in aggravated

**On average, the juvenile arrest rate for aggravated assault declined 5% each year since 1994**

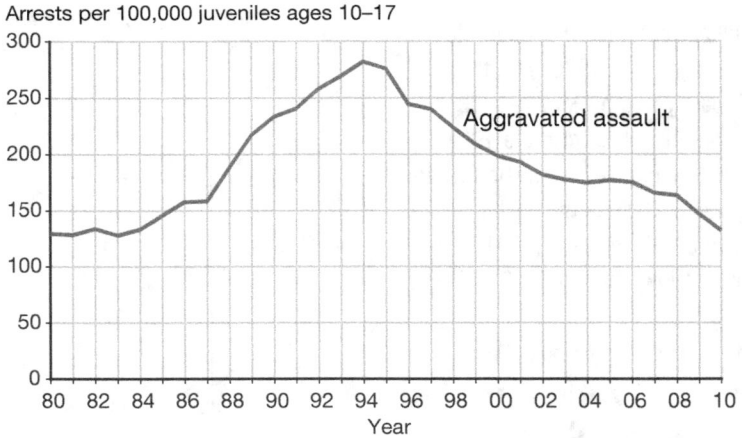

### Aggravated assault arrest rate trends by gender and race

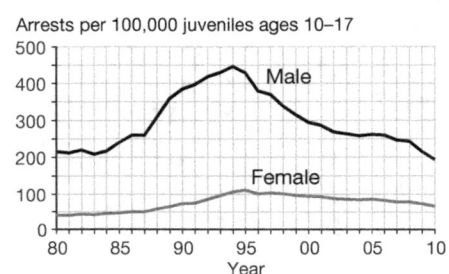
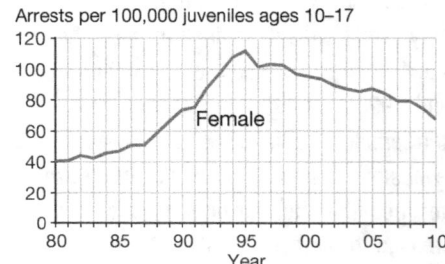
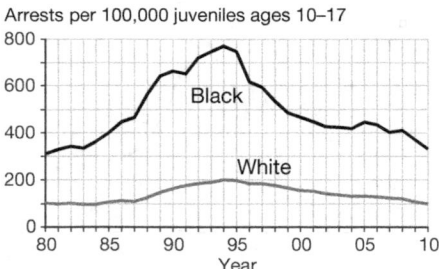
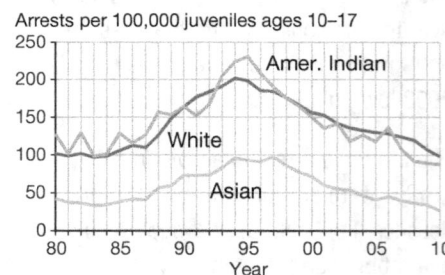

■ The black-white disparity in aggravated assault arrest rates peaked in 1988, when the black rate was more than 4 times the white rate; by 2010, this black-white ratio was a little more than 3-to-1.

**Data source:** Analysis of arrest data from the Bureau of Justice Statistics, and population data from the U.S. Bureau of the Census. (See arrest rate data source note on page 23 for details.)

assault arrest rates for juveniles in each racial group: black (149% increase), Asian (126%), white (97%), and American Indian (73%). Rates have declined for all racial groups since the mid 1990s, so much so that rates in 2010 were at their lowest levels since the early 1980s.

# The juvenile arrest rate for property crimes in 2010 was at its lowest point since at least 1980

## Juvenile property crime arrest rates have fallen almost continuously since 1994

Between 1980 and 1994, the juvenile arrest rate for Property Crime Index offenses varied little, always remaining within 10% of the average for the period. After years of relative stability, the juvenile Property Crime Index arrest rate began a decline in the mid-1990s that continued annually until reaching a then-historic low in 2006, down 54% from its 1988 peak. This nearly two-decade decline was followed by a 10% increase over the next 2 years, and then a 15% decline between 2008 and 2010. As a result, juveniles were far less likely to be arrested for property crimes in 2010 than they were 30 years earlier.

## Female property crime arrest rates increased since 2006

In 1980, the juvenile male arrest rate for Property Crime Index offenses was 4 times the female rate; by 2010, the male rate was about 60% above the female rate. These two rates converged in large part because the female rate increased 25% between 2006 and 2009, whereas the male rate declined 3%. The stark differences in the male and female trends suggest several possibilities, including gender-specific changes in these behaviors and an increased willingness to arrest female offenders.

The Property Crime Index arrest rates in 2010 were at their lowest level in 31 years for white, American Indian, and Asian youth, while the rate for black youth in 2010 was just 2% above its 2006 low point. In the 31 years from 1980 to 2010, the black youth arrest rate for property

**The juvenile Property Crime Index arrest rate fell 15% between 2008 and 2010, erasing the increase between 2006 and 2008**

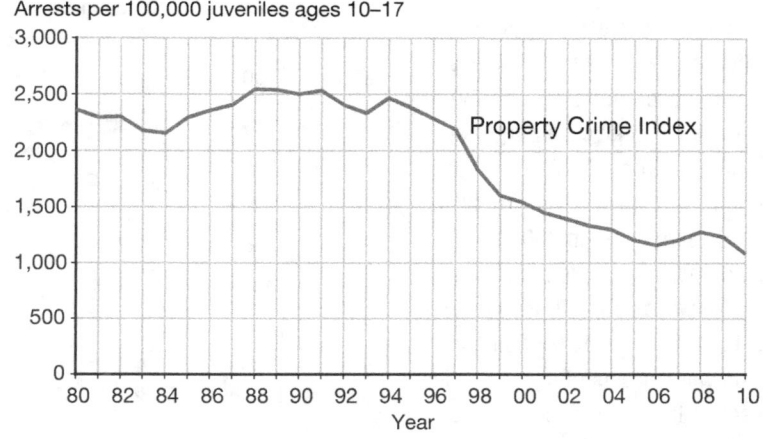

### Property Crime Index arrest rate trends by gender and race

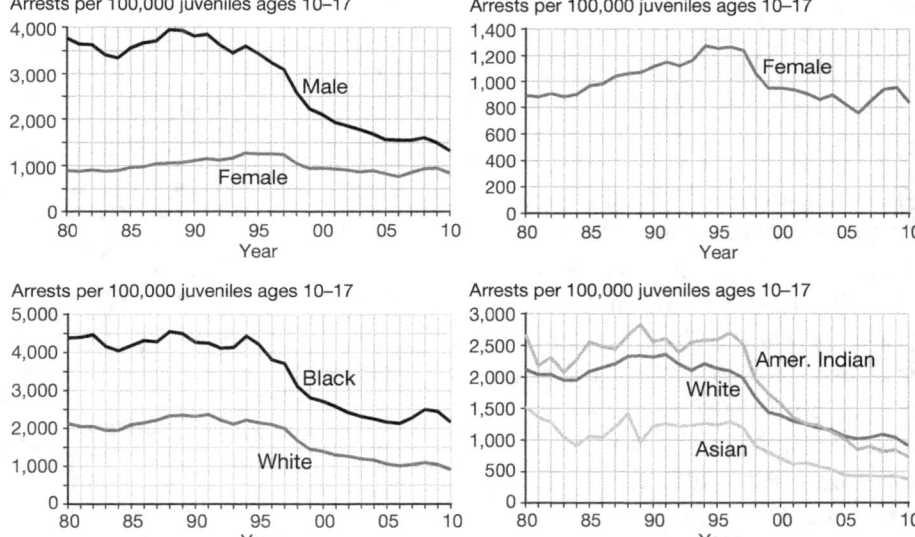

- In 2010, for every 100,000 youth in the United States ages 10–17, there were 1,084 arrests of juveniles for Property Crime Index offenses. The Property Crime Index is dominated by larceny-theft, which in 2010 contributed 77% of all juvenile Property Crime Index arrests. Therefore, the trends in Property Crime Index arrests largely reflect the trends in arrests for larceny-theft.

**Data source:** Analysis of arrest data from the Bureau of Justice Statistics, and population data from the U.S. Bureau of the Census. (See arrest rate data source note on page 23 for details.)

crimes averaged twice the white youth rate, much smaller than the black-white disparity in juvenile arrest rates for violent crimes.

# The juvenile arrest rate for burglary in 2010 was at its lowest rate since at least 1980

## Juvenile arrests for burglary fell more than adult arrests

In 2010, the juvenile arrest rate for burglary reached its lowest point in the past 31 years, nearly one-quarter of its 1980 level. This large fall in juvenile burglary arrests from 1980 through 2010 was not replicated in the adult statistics. For example, in the 10 years between 2001 and 2010, the number of juvenile burglary arrests fell 27%, while adult burglary arrests increased 11%. In 1980, 45% of all burglary arrests were arrests of a juvenile; in 2010, reflecting the greater decline in juvenile arrests, just 23% of burglary arrests were juvenile arrests.

## Juvenile female arrest rates for burglary declined less than male rates

The substantial decline in the juvenile burglary arrest rate was primarily the result of a decline in juvenile male arrests. In 1980, 6% of juveniles arrested for burglary were female; by 2010, 11% were female. Between 1980 and 2010, the male rate fell 75%, while the female rate dropped 52%. As a result of these declines, both rates in 2010 were at their lowest level since 1980.

## Juvenile burglary arrest rates fell for all racial groups

Between 1980 and 2010, the juvenile burglary arrest rate declined for all racial groups: 88% for Asians and American Indians, 76% for whites, and 67% for blacks. As a result, rates for Asian, American Indian, and white youth in 2010 were at their lowest levels of the 31-year period and the rate for black youth was 7% above its 2004 low point.

**Unique in the set of property crime offenses, the juvenile arrest rate for burglary declined almost consistently and fell 74% between 1980 and 2010**

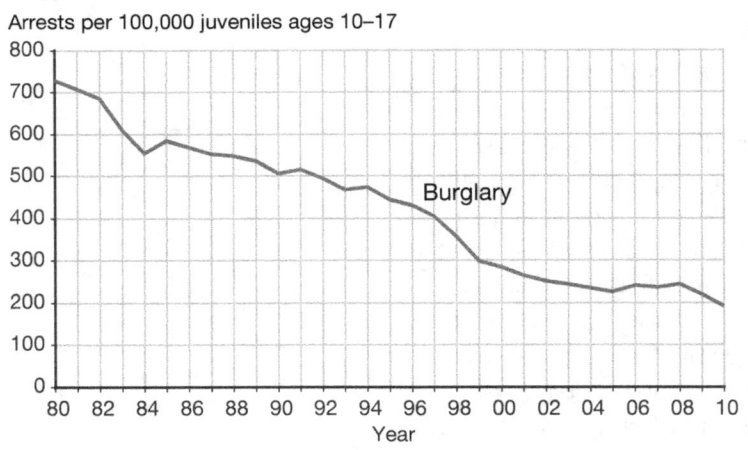

Arrests per 100,000 juveniles ages 10–17

### Burglary arrest rate trends by gender and race

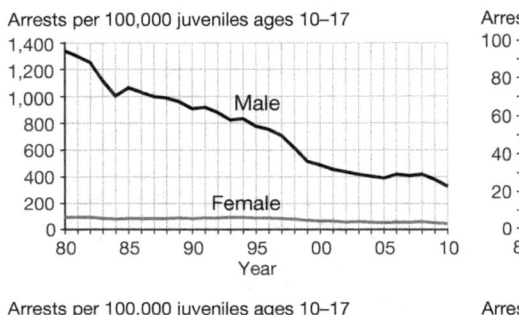

Arrests per 100,000 juveniles ages 10–17

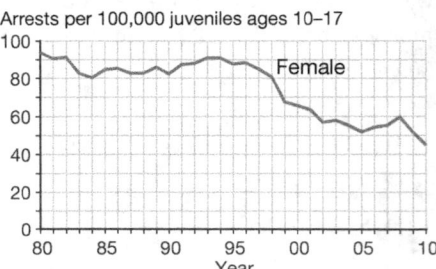

Arrests per 100,000 juveniles ages 10–17

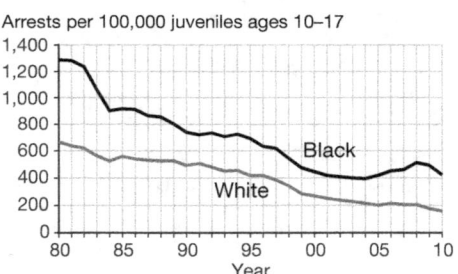

Arrests per 100,000 juveniles ages 10–17

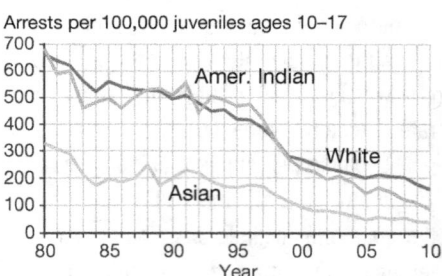

Arrests per 100,000 juveniles ages 10–17

■ The gender disparity in juvenile burglary arrest rates has diminished over the past 31 years. In 1980, the juvenile male arrest rate for burglary was more than 14 times the female rate; in 2010, the male rate was 7 times the female rate.

**Data source:** Analysis of arrest data from the Bureau of Justice Statistics, and population data from the U.S. Bureau of the Census. (See arrest rate data source note on page 23 for details.)

# Despite recent growth, juvenile arrest rates for larceny-theft remain low

## The 2010 juvenile larceny-theft rate was about half the rates of the 1980s and 1990s

The juvenile arrest rate for larceny-theft generally increased between 1980 and the mid-1990s and then fell 52% between 1994 and 2006, reaching its lowest point since 1980. This decline reversed as the juvenile arrest rate for larceny-theft increased 4% between 2006 and 2010. Despite this increase, the overall decline in arrests for a high-volume offense translated into significantly fewer juveniles charged with property crimes entering the justice system.

## The female proportion of larceny-theft arrests has grown

In 1980, 26% of juveniles arrested for larceny-theft were female; by 2010, this proportion had grown to 45%. Although larceny-theft arrest rates dropped for male and female juveniles in the late 1990s and early 2000s, the prior increases for females resulted in their 2006 rate being just 11% below their 1980 rate, whereas the 2006 rate for males was 55% below their 1980 rate. By 2010, the rate for males reached its lowest point since at least 1980, while the female rate was 16% above its 2006 low point.

The decline in the juvenile arrest rate for larceny-theft between 1994 and 2006 was similar in each of the four racial groups: 66% each for Asians and American Indians, 53% for whites, and 52% for blacks. Since 2006, the black juvenile larceny-theft arrest rate increased 15%, while the rates for other racial groups remained about the same. In 2010, the black

**The recent increase in the juvenile arrest rate for larceny-theft reversed in 2010, as the rate fell 11% from the previous year**

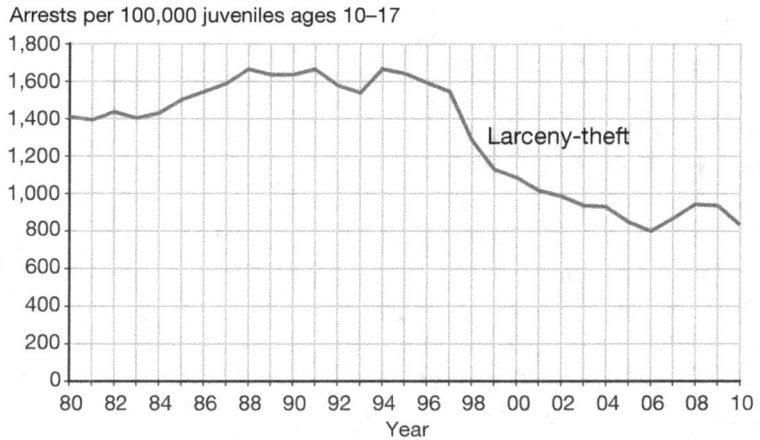

### Larceny-theft arrest rate trends by gender and race

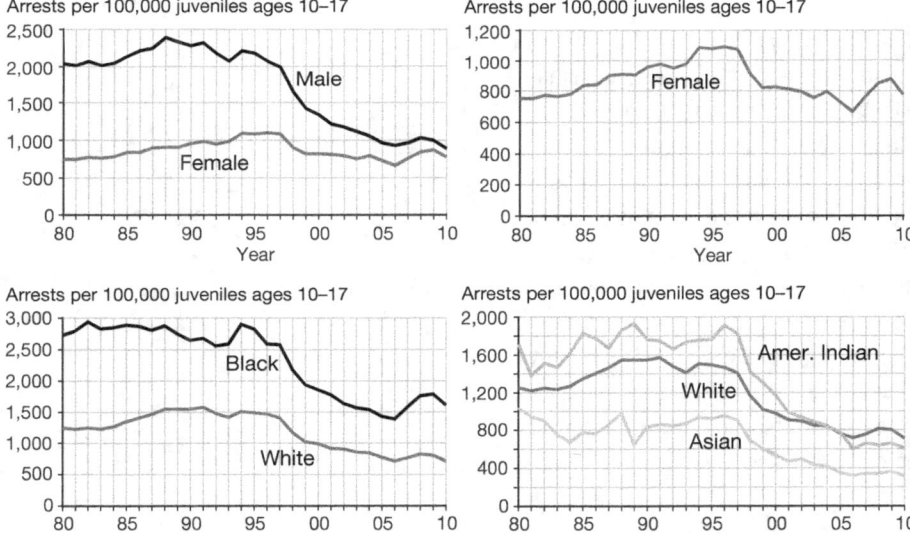

- Larceny-theft is the unlawful taking of property from the possession of another. This crime group includes such offenses as shoplifting, bicycle theft, and pickpocketing—or thefts without the use of force, threat, or fraud. For juveniles, it has been the most common type of crime: in 2010, 1 in 5 juvenile arrests was for larceny-theft.

**Data source:** Analysis of arrest data from the Bureau of Justice Statistics, and population data from the U.S. Bureau of the Census. (See arrest rate data source note on page 23 for details.)

juvenile larceny-theft arrest rate was 2.3 times greater than the white juvenile rate, equivalent to the 1982 peak in black-white disparity for larceny-theft.

# The motor vehicle theft arrest rate for juveniles was at a 31-year low in 2010

## The juvenile arrest rate for motor vehicle theft peaked in 1989

The juvenile arrest rate for motor vehicle theft more than doubled between 1983 and 1989, up 141%. After the 1989 peak, the juvenile arrest rate for motor vehicle theft declined steadily, erasing its prior growth by the early 2000s. In 2010, the juvenile arrest rate for motor vehicle theft was lower than in any year in the 31-year period, 86% below its peak level. This large decline in juvenile arrests outpaced declines in adult statistics. In the 10-year period between 2001 and 2010, the number of juvenile motor vehicle theft arrests fell 67%, and adult motor vehicle theft arrests decreased 44%.

Male and female juvenile arrest rates for motor vehicle theft displayed generally similar trends in the 1980s and 1990s, first increasing and then decreasing. However, the male rate peaked in 1989, but the female rate did not peak until 1994. With a longer period of decline than the female rate, the male rate in 1999 fell to within 1% of its 1983 level, but the female rate was still 66% above this low point. By 2010, the male and female rates reached their lowest level in over three decades.

From 1983 to their peak years, arrest rates for motor vehicle theft nearly doubled for white juveniles (peak year 1990) and Asian juveniles (peak year 1988), increased nearly 150% for American Indian juveniles (peak year 1989), and more than tripled for black juveniles (peak year 1989). By 2010, motor vehicle theft arrest rates were at their lowest level since at least 1980 for all race groups.

**Between 1989 and 2010, the juvenile arrest rate for motor vehicle theft fell 86%, so that the rate in 2010 was at its lowest level since 1980**

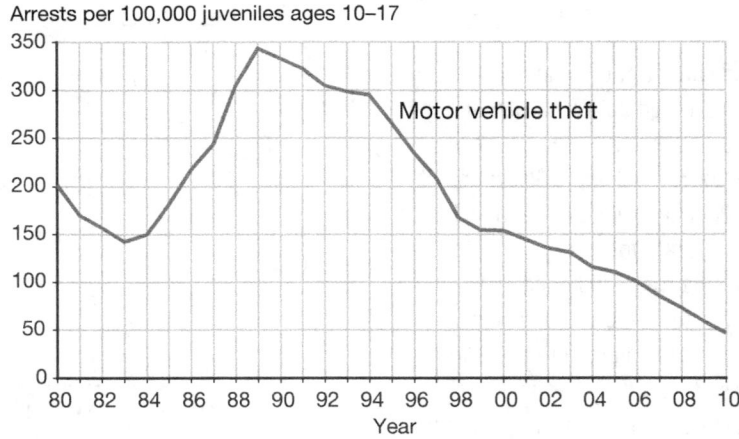

Arrests per 100,000 juveniles ages 10–17

### Motor vehicle theft arrest rate trends by gender and race

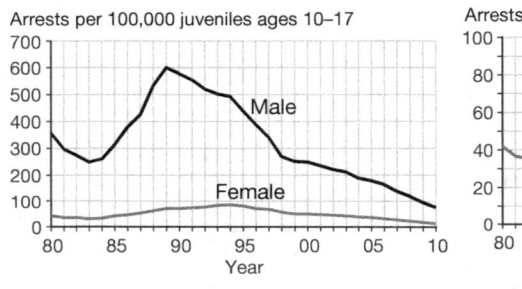

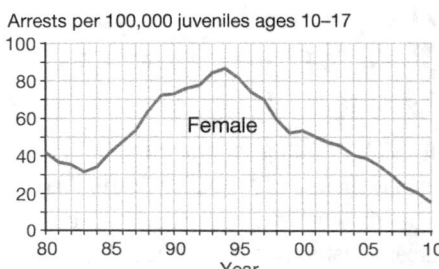

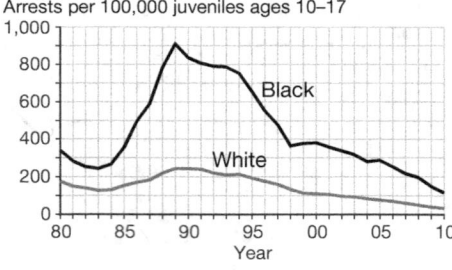

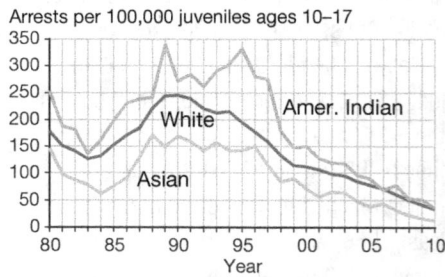

- The juvenile arrest rate trends for motor vehicle theft differed from those for the other high-volume theft crimes of burglary and larceny-theft. In the 1980s and 1990s, the burglary arrest rate declined consistently and the larceny-theft rate remained relatively stable, but the motor vehicle theft rate soared and then dropped just as dramatically.

**Data source:** Analysis of arrest data from the Bureau of Justice Statistics, and population data from the U.S. Bureau of the Census. (See arrest rate data source note on page 23 for details.)

# Forty percent of all persons arrested for arson in 2010 were younger than 18; 1 in 4 was younger than 15

## Arson is the criminal act with the largest proportion of juvenile arrestees

In 2010, 40% of all arson arrests were arrests of juveniles, and most of these juvenile arrests (58%) involved youth younger than 15. In comparison, 22% of all larceny-theft arrests in 2010 involved juveniles, but only 28% of these juvenile arrests involved youth younger than 15.

## Trends in juvenile arson arrests paralleled that of violent crime

The pattern of stability, growth, and decline in the juvenile arrest rate for arson in the past 31 years was similar in magnitude and character to the trend in juvenile violent crime arrest rates. After years of stability, the juvenile arrest rate for arson increased more than 50% between 1987 and 1994 before falling 60% through 2010. During the period of increase, the female rate increased abruptly between 1991 and 1994 (up 66%). During the period of decline after 1994, the male and female rates declined proportionally (63% and 59%, respectively). However, because of the greater increase in the female rate, these declines left the female rate in 2010 32% below its 1980 level, and the male rate was 48% below its 1980 level.

One major distinction between violent crime and arson arrest rates over this period was that white and black rates were similar for arson but not for violent crime. Between 1980 and 2010, on average, the black rate was 5% greater than the white rate for arson, but the violent crime arrest rate for black juveniles was 5 times the white rate. For white juveniles and black juveniles, arson arrest rates were essentially equal for most years between 1980 and 1992. After 1992, the black rate rose to slightly above the white rate; however, both groups ended the 31-year period at their lowest rates.

**Following a 42% decline between 2006 and 2010, the juvenile arrest rate for arson in 2010 reached a historic low**

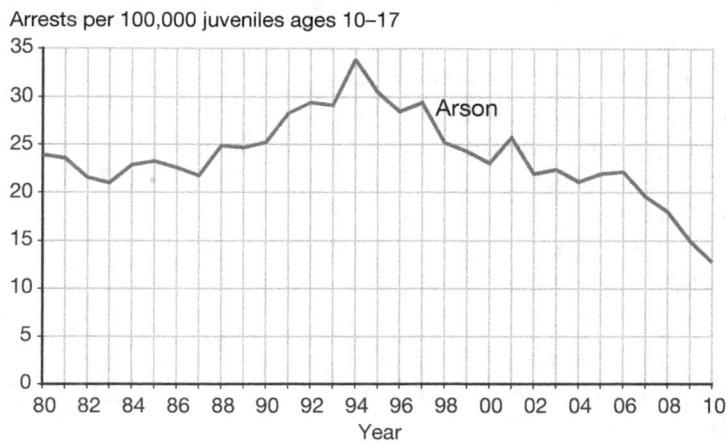

### Arson arrest rate trends by gender and race

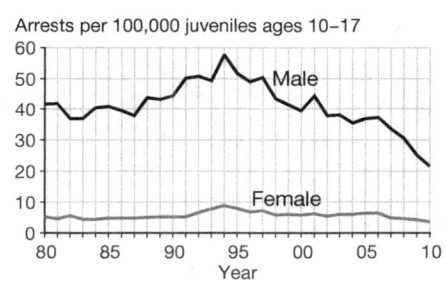

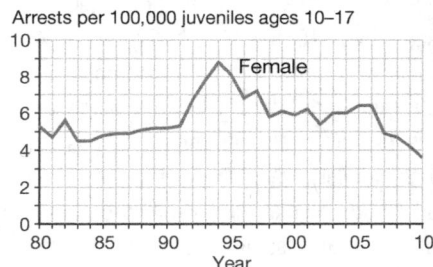

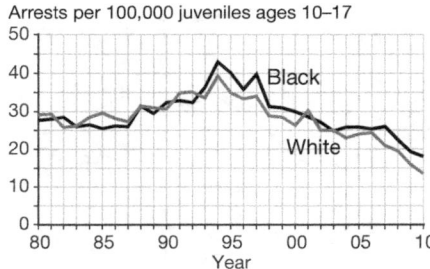

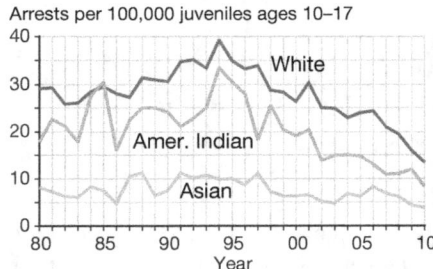

■ Between 1980 and 2010, the arson arrest rate for Asian juveniles stayed within a limited range and was substantially below the rate for other races, averaging less than 30% of the white rate over the 31-year period.

**Data source:** Analysis of arrest data from the Bureau of Justice Statistics, and population data from the U.S. Bureau of the Census. (See arrest rate data source note on page 23 for details.)

# The juvenile arrest rate for simple assault in 2010 was more than twice the 1980 rate

## Simple assault is the most common of all crimes against persons

The juvenile arrest rate for simple assault increased 176% between 1980 and 1997, declined through 2002, then rose again through 2004. Following the decline since 2004, the 2010 rate was 19% below the 1997 peak. Unlike the trend for simple assault, the juvenile aggravated assault arrest rate declined steadily between 1994 and 2010, falling 53%. As a result of these divergent trends, a greater percentage of assaults that law enforcement handled in recent years has been for less serious offenses. In 1980, there were 2 juvenile arrests for simple assault for every 1 juvenile arrest for aggravated assault; by 2010, this ratio had grown to 4-to-1—with most of this growth occurring after the mid-1990s. The large increase in the juvenile arrest rate for simple assault was paralleled by a similar increase in the adult rate, so that the juvenile proportion of all simple assault arrests was 18% in 1980 and 16% in 2010.

## Growth in the female arrest rate for simple assault outpaced the male rate

As with aggravated assault, between 1980 and 2010, the increase in the juvenile female arrest rate for simple assault far outpaced the increase in the male rate (278% vs. 83%). As a result, the female proportion of juvenile arrests for simple assault grew from 21% to 35%. During that period, simple assault arrest rates increased substantially for black (131%), white (114%), and American Indian (38%) youth, with rates for Asian youth declining 15% over the 31-year period. These increases were greater than the corresponding increases in aggravated assault rates.

### The juvenile arrest rate for simple assault has declined steadily since 2004—down 15% over that period

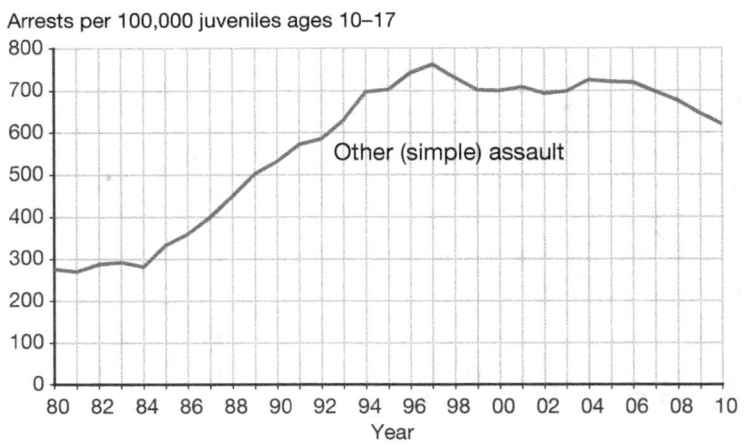

### Other (simple) assault arrest rate trends by gender and race

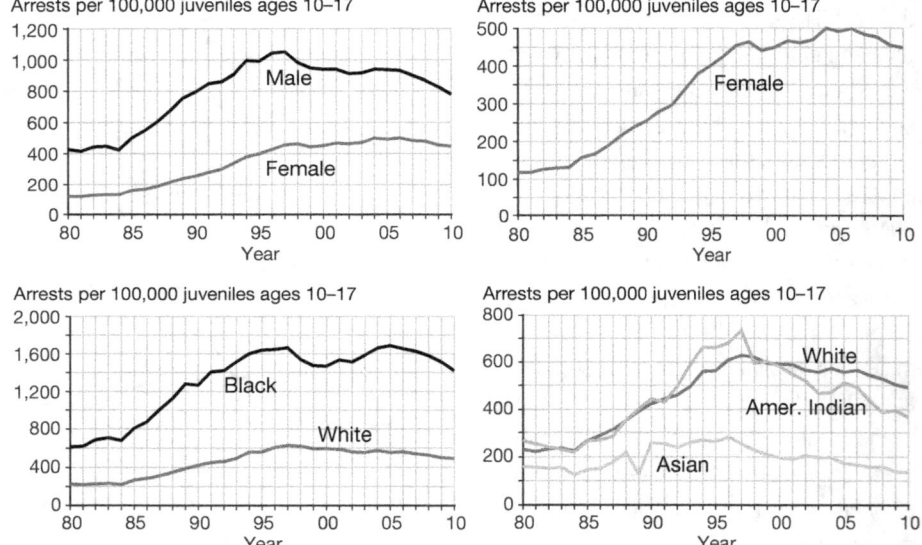

- Juvenile male and female simple assault arrest rates declined similarly between 2006 and 2010 (by 16% and 10%, respectively).

- In 2010, the ratio of simple to aggravated assault arrests of juveniles varied across gender and racial groups: male (4.0-to-1), female (6.7-to-1), white (5.0-to-1), black (4.3-to-1), American Indian (4.2-to-1), and Asian (5.0-to-1).

**Note:** In contrast to aggravated assault, a simple assault does not involve the use of a weapon and does not result in serious bodily harm to the victim. The lesser severity of simple assault makes the reporting of it to law enforcement less likely and gives law enforcement more discretion in how they handle the incident.

**Data source:** Analysis of arrest data from the Bureau of Justice Statistics, and population data from the U.S. Bureau of the Census. (See arrest rate data source note on page 23 for details.)

# Juvenile arrest rate trends for weapons law violations generally paralleled trends for violent crimes

## The juvenile weapons arrest rate in 2010 was half its 1994 peak

Between 1980 and 1994, the juvenile arrest rate for weapons law violations increased 146%. Then the rate fell substantially, so that by 2002 the rate was just 21% more than the 1980 level. However, between 2002 and 2006, the juvenile weapons arrest rate grew 32% and then fell 32% through 2010. As a result, the rate in 2010 was 8% above the 1980 level and 56% below its 1994 peak. It must be remembered that these statistics do not reflect all arrests for weapons offenses. An unknown number of other arrests for more serious crimes also involved a weapons offense as a secondary charge, but the FBI's arrest statistics classify such arrests by their most serious charge and not the weapons offense.

Between 1980 and 1994, the arrest rate for weapons law violations increased proportionally more for females (256%) than for males (139%). After reaching a peak in 1994, both rates declined through 2002 (53% for males and 32% for females), increased through 2006, and then fell through 2010.

Arrest rates for weapons law violations peaked in 1993 for black juveniles, in 1994 for white and Asian juveniles, and in 1995 for American Indian juveniles. The increase between 1980 and the peak year was the greatest for black juveniles (215%), followed by whites (126%), Asians (104%), and American Indians (83%). Similar to trends for males and females, the rates for all racial groups dropped quickly after their peaks, grew between 2002 and 2006, and fell again between 2006 and 2010. Despite recent declines, the 2010 arrest rates were still slightly above their 1980 levels for male

### The juvenile arrest rate for weapons law violations declined for the fourth consecutive year, falling 32% since 2006

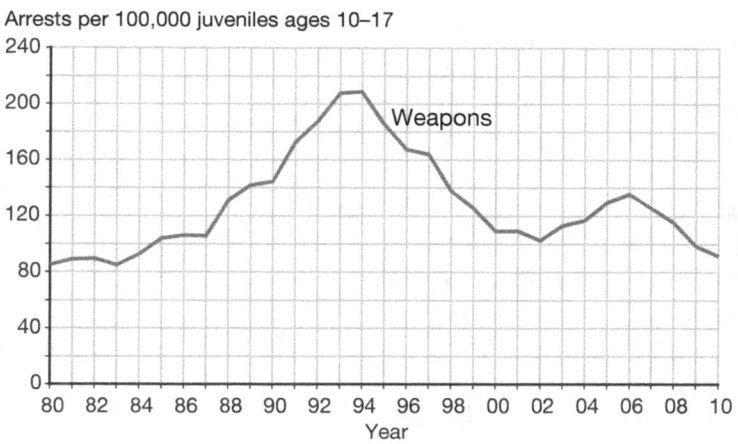

### Weapons law violation arrest rate trends by gender and race

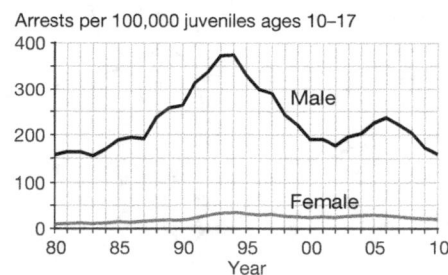
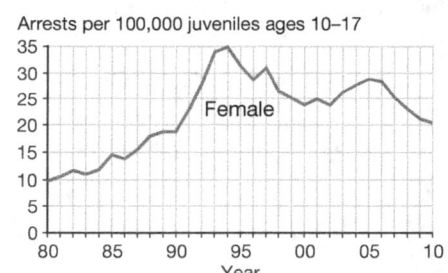
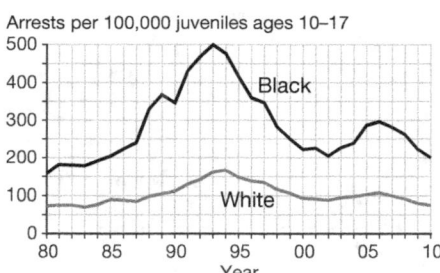
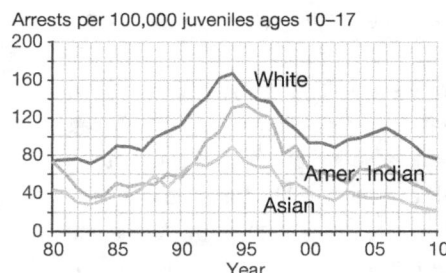

■ The disproportionate increase in the female rate narrowed the gender disparity in weapons law violation arrest rates. In 1980, the male rate was 16 times the female rate; in 2010, the male rate was about 8 times the female rate.

**Data source:** Analysis of arrest data from the Bureau of Justice Statistics, and population data from the U.S. Bureau of the Census. (See arrest rate data source note on page 23 for details.)

(2%) and white (3%) juveniles, and substantially above their 1980 levels for female (109%) and black (27%) juveniles. In 2010, arrest rates for weapons law violations were actually below their 1980 levels for American Indian and Asian youth (by 49% and 50%, respectively).

# The juvenile drug arrest rate more than doubled between 1991 and 1997 but has since declined

## Racial disparity in drug arrests increased in the 1980s and early 1990s

The annual juvenile arrest rates for drug abuse violations (a category that includes both drug possession and drug sales) varied within a limited range in the 1980s. A closer look at juvenile drug arrest rates finds sharp racial differences. The drug abuse violation arrest rate for white juveniles generally declined between 1980 and 1991, while the black rate soared. The white rate fell 54%, compared with a 190% increase for blacks. In 1980, the white and black arrest rates were essentially equal, with black youth involved in 14% of all juvenile drug arrests. By 1991, the black rate was nearly 6 times the white rate, and black youth were involved in 52% of all juvenile drug arrests.

## Drug arrests soared for all youth between 1991 and 1997

Between 1991 and 1997, the juvenile arrest rate for drug abuse violations increased 138%. The rate declined 26% between 1997 and 2010, but the 2010 rate was 76% more than the 1991 rate. After a period of substantial growth through the 1990s, the male juvenile arrest rate for drug abuse violations generally declined after 1996, while the female rate remained relatively stable. By 2010, the drug abuse arrest rate for males declined 29% from its 1996 peak, whereas the rate for females was just 7% below its 1996 level. For both groups, the arrest rates in 2010 were considerably above the rates in 1980 (41% for both males and females). Between 1980 and 2010, the juvenile drug arrest rate for whites peaked in 1997 and then remained relatively constant through 2010 (down 14%). In contrast, the rate for blacks peaked in 1996

and then fell 41% by 2002. Despite a recent increase—15% between 2002 and

2006—the rate fell 22% through 2010 and was 52% less than the 1996 peak.

### After a period of substantial growth through the 1990s, the juvenile arrest rate for drug abuse violations generally declined through 2010

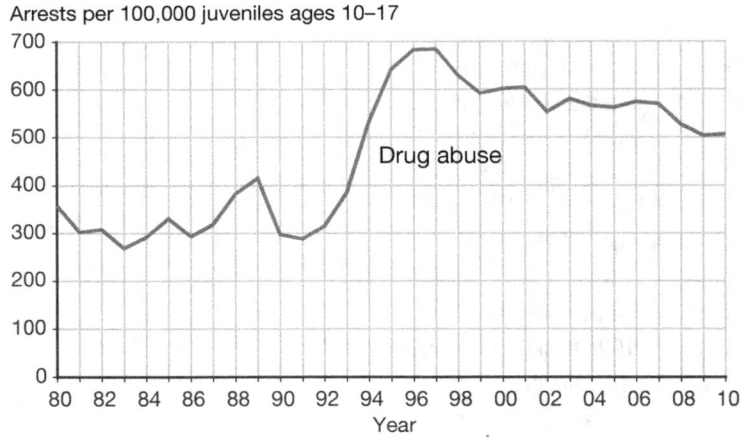

Arrests per 100,000 juveniles ages 10–17

### Drug abuse violation arrest rate trends by gender and race

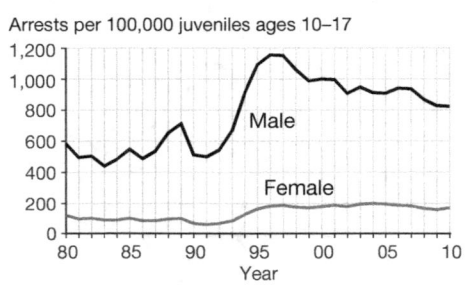

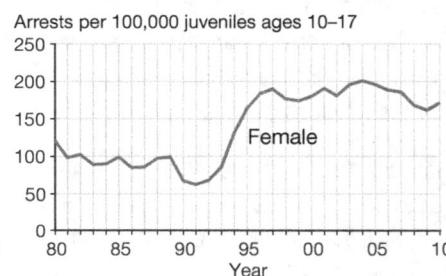

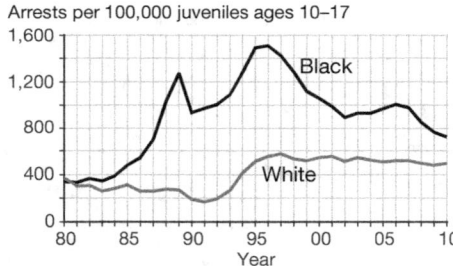

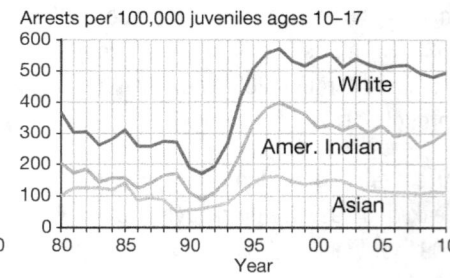

■ The trend in juvenile arrests for drug abuse violations among blacks was different from the trends for other racial groups. Whereas the arrest rate for other races generally declined throughout the 1980s, the rate for black juveniles increased substantially during this period.

■ Despite recent declines, rates for all racial groups in 2010 remained above their 1980 rates: white (34%), black (115%), American Indian (49%), and Asian (9%).

**Data source:** Analysis of arrest data from the Bureau of Justice Statistics, and population data from the U.S. Bureau of the Census. (See arrest rate data source note on page 23 for details.)

# In 2010, more than one-fourth of states had a juvenile violent crime arrest rate above the national average

**Among states with at least minimally adequate reporting, those with high juvenile violent crime arrest rates in 2010 were California, Delaware, Florida, Louisiana, Maryland, Pennsylvania, and Tennessee**

| State | Reporting population coverage | Arrests of juveniles under age 18 per 100,000 juveniles ages 10–17 | | | | | State | Reporting population coverage | Arrests of juveniles under age 18 per 100,000 juveniles ages 10–17 | | | | |
| | | Violent Crime Index | Robbery | Aggrav. assault | Other assault | Weapon | | | Violent Crime Index | Robbery | Aggrav. assault | Other assault | Weapon |
|---|---|---|---|---|---|---|---|---|---|---|---|---|---|
| U.S. total | 84% | 225 | 81 | 132 | 619 | 92 | Missouri | 93% | 222 | 68 | 142 | 901 | 70 |
| Alabama | 72 | 80 | 27 | 48 | 229 | 19 | Montana | 87 | 120 | 16 | 97 | 647 | 23 |
| Alaska | 99 | 248 | 50 | 192 | 539 | 35 | Nebraska | 90 | 109 | 42 | 50 | 1,081 | 86 |
| Arizona | 90 | 182 | 41 | 133 | 635 | 49 | Nevada | 89 | 300 | 112 | 180 | 944 | 105 |
| Arkansas | 74 | 130 | 23 | 96 | 612 | 49 | New Hampshire | 87 | 93 | 23 | 62 | 940 | 17 |
| California | 96 | 304 | 123 | 172 | 417 | 162 | New Jersey | 98 | 243 | 114 | 119 | 326 | 118 |
| Colorado | 89 | 156 | 31 | 111 | 409 | 90 | New Mexico | 88 | 240 | 22 | 200 | 854 | 120 |
| Connecticut | 95 | 212 | 75 | 126 | 1,007 | 66 | New York | 50 | 221 | 90 | 121 | 494 | 58 |
| Delaware | 100 | 368 | 117 | 230 | 1,287 | 127 | North Carolina | 83 | 211 | 73 | 122 | 850 | 172 |
| Dist. of Columbia | 0 | NA | NA | NA | NA | NA | North Dakota | 90 | 92 | 9 | 58 | 636 | 22 |
| Florida | 100 | 343 | 110 | 218 | 759 | 67 | Ohio | 74 | 111 | 60 | 41 | 669 | 54 |
| Georgia | 81 | 192 | 65 | 117 | 618 | 104 | Oklahoma | 99 | 149 | 34 | 104 | 293 | 65 |
| Hawaii | 89 | 217 | 108 | 96 | 778 | 18 | Oregon | 87 | 147 | 47 | 93 | 469 | 55 |
| Idaho | 94 | 93 | 10 | 72 | 628 | 77 | Pennsylvania | 97 | 355 | 135 | 202 | 619 | 99 |
| Illinois | 23 | 815 | 379 | 411 | 1,247 | 275 | Rhode Island | 99 | 198 | 69 | 110 | 684 | 145 |
| Indiana | 59 | 143 | 32 | 105 | 607 | 50 | South Carolina | 95 | 186 | 48 | 124 | 692 | 114 |
| Iowa | 88 | 203 | 23 | 171 | 785 | 40 | South Dakota | 78 | 109 | 10 | 90 | 679 | 97 |
| Kansas | 69 | 149 | 20 | 115 | 541 | 37 | Tennessee | 78 | 383 | 100 | 268 | 1,052 | 120 |
| Kentucky | 70 | 125 | 62 | 53 | 326 | 33 | Texas | 99 | 146 | 46 | 90 | 737 | 40 |
| Louisiana | 58 | 503 | 72 | 408 | 1,105 | 82 | Utah | 97 | 90 | 18 | 56 | 609 | 99 |
| Maine | 100 | 55 | 15 | 34 | 688 | 44 | Vermont | 87 | 66 | 0 | 40 | 340 | 9 |
| Maryland | 83 | 522 | 261 | 249 | 1,303 | 185 | Virginia | 98 | 112 | 47 | 58 | 622 | 53 |
| Massachusetts | 94 | 259 | 52 | 200 | 384 | 35 | Washington | 78 | 211 | 77 | 118 | 681 | 92 |
| Michigan | 94 | 179 | 63 | 104 | 387 | 63 | West Virginia | 80 | 59 | 11 | 44 | 248 | 8 |
| Minnesota | 100 | 160 | 54 | 104 | 574 | 92 | Wisconsin | 89 | 237 | 103 | 106 | 502 | 153 |
| Mississippi | 53 | 119 | 71 | 34 | 748 | 125 | Wyoming | 99 | 96 | 16 | 77 | 1,080 | 82 |

NA = Arrest counts were not available for the District of Columbia in the FBI's *Crime in the United States 2010.*

**Notes:** Arrest rates for jurisdictions with less than complete reporting may not be representative of the entire state. In the map, rates were classified as "Data not available" when agencies with jurisdiction over more than 50% of their state's population did not report. Readers should consult the related technical note on page 23. Detail may not add to totals because of rounding.

**Data source:** Analysis of arrest data from *Crime in the United States 2010* (Washington, DC: Federal Bureau of Investigation, 2011) tables 5 and 69, and population data from the National Center for Health Statistics' *Postcensal Estimates of the Resident Population of the United States for July 1, 2010–July 1, 2011, by Year, County, Single-Year of Age (0, 1, 2, . . ., 85 Years and Over), Bridged Race, Hispanic Origin, and Sex (Vintage 2011)* [machine-readable data files available online at www.cdc.gov/nchs/nvss/bridged_race.htm, as of 7/18/12].

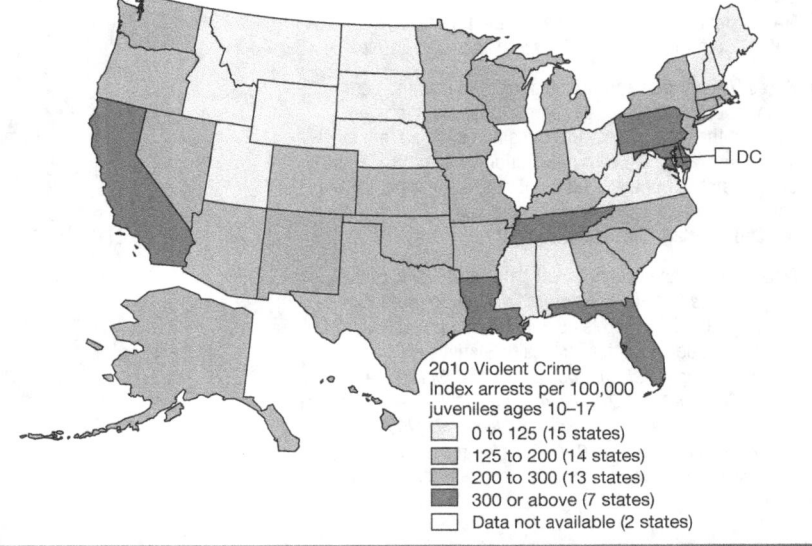

2010 Violent Crime Index arrests per 100,000 juveniles ages 10–17

☐ 0 to 125 (15 states)
☐ 125 to 200 (14 states)
☐ 200 to 300 (13 states)
☐ 300 or above (7 states)
☐ Data not available (2 states)

# High juvenile violent crime arrest rates in 2010 did not necessarily mean high property crime arrest rates

**Among states with at least minimally adequate reporting, those with high juvenile property crime arrest rates in 2010 were Nebraska, South Dakota, and Wisconsin**

| State | Reporting population coverage | Arrests of juveniles under age 18 per 100,000 juveniles ages 10–17 Property Crime Index | Burglary | Larceny-theft | Motor vehicle theft | Vandalism | State | Reporting population coverage | Arrests of juveniles under age 18 per 100,000 juveniles ages 10–17 Property Crime Index | Burglary | Larceny-theft | Motor vehicle theft | Vandalism |
|---|---|---|---|---|---|---|---|---|---|---|---|---|---|
| U.S. total | 84% | 1,084 | 192 | 832 | 47 | 13 | Missouri | 93% | 1,537 | 219 | 1,254 | 53 | 12 |
| Alabama | 72 | 495 | 69 | 412 | 12 | 2 | Montana | 87 | 1,570 | 90 | 1,374 | 84 | 22 |
| Alaska | 99 | 1,329 | 170 | 1,063 | 72 | 24 | Nebraska | 90 | 1,920 | 146 | 1,700 | 57 | 17 |
| Arizona | 90 | 1,426 | 190 | 1,176 | 44 | 17 | Nevada | 89 | 1,492 | 215 | 1,235 | 28 | 14 |
| Arkansas | 74 | 984 | 174 | 790 | 14 | 6 | New Hampshire | 87 | 825 | 97 | 691 | 21 | 17 |
| California | 96 | 922 | 293 | 560 | 56 | 13 | New Jersey | 98 | 736 | 119 | 585 | 16 | 16 |
| Colorado | 89 | 1,424 | 121 | 1,228 | 52 | 24 | New Mexico | 88 | 1,488 | 169 | 1,241 | 56 | 23 |
| Connecticut | 95 | 849 | 131 | 663 | 40 | 15 | New York | 50 | 1,084 | 194 | 833 | 47 | 10 |
| Delaware | 100 | 1,452 | 299 | 1,098 | 44 | 12 | North Carolina | 83 | 1,177 | 321 | 818 | 25 | 14 |
| Dist. of Columbia | 0 | NA | NA | NA | NA | NA | North Dakota | 90 | 1,693 | 116 | 1,490 | 80 | 7 |
| Florida | 100 | 1,530 | 426 | 1,023 | 74 | 8 | Ohio | 74 | 771 | 138 | 595 | 29 | 9 |
| Georgia | 81 | 1,200 | 244 | 891 | 56 | 9 | Oklahoma | 99 | 1,167 | 190 | 924 | 23 | 29 |
| Hawaii | 89 | 1,284 | 87 | 1,129 | 55 | 13 | Oregon | 87 | 1,635 | 157 | 1,387 | 48 | 42 |
| Idaho | 94 | 1,456 | 198 | 1,197 | 38 | 23 | Pennsylvania | 97 | 874 | 135 | 671 | 49 | 19 |
| Illinois | 23 | 1,449 | 307 | 808 | 330 | 5 | Rhode Island | 99 | 901 | 217 | 617 | 37 | 30 |
| Indiana | 59 | 1,198 | 138 | 1,013 | 40 | 7 | South Carolina | 95 | 1,110 | 212 | 865 | 29 | 4 |
| Iowa | 88 | 1,616 | 241 | 1,305 | 47 | 23 | South Dakota | 78 | 1,818 | 110 | 1,646 | 53 | 9 |
| Kansas | 69 | 976 | 110 | 807 | 44 | 15 | Tennessee | 78 | 1,352 | 276 | 995 | 63 | 18 |
| Kentucky | 70 | 754 | 162 | 565 | 20 | 7 | Texas | 99 | 1,049 | 161 | 854 | 28 | 6 |
| Louisiana | 58 | 1,517 | 299 | 1,156 | 51 | 11 | Utah | 97 | 1,748 | 96 | 1,610 | 31 | 11 |
| Maine | 100 | 1,346 | 267 | 991 | 54 | 34 | Vermont | 87 | 469 | 107 | 312 | 33 | 17 |
| Maryland | 83 | 1,697 | 287 | 1,251 | 127 | 32 | Virginia | 98 | 763 | 101 | 621 | 26 | 14 |
| Massachusetts | 94 | 449 | 98 | 319 | 21 | 11 | Washington | 78 | 1,201 | 202 | 934 | 49 | 16 |
| Michigan | 94 | 880 | 151 | 662 | 54 | 13 | West Virginia | 80 | 346 | 39 | 288 | 15 | 4 |
| Minnesota | 100 | 1,507 | 137 | 1,312 | 40 | 17 | Wisconsin | 89 | 1,904 | 222 | 1,607 | 63 | 12 |
| Mississippi | 53 | 1,350 | 367 | 941 | 36 | 7 | Wyoming | 99 | 1,636 | 197 | 1,378 | 47 | 14 |

NA = Arrest counts were not available for the District of Columbia in the FBI's *Crime in the United States 2010.*

**Notes:** Arrest rates for jurisdictions with less than complete reporting may not be representative of the entire state. In the map, rates were classified as "Data not available" when agencies with jurisdiction over more than 50% of their state's population did not report. Readers should consult the related technical note on page 23. Detail may not add to totals because of rounding.

**Data source:** Analysis of arrest data from *Crime in the United States 2010* (Washington, DC: Federal Bureau of Investigation, 2011) tables 5 and 69, and population data from the National Center for Health Statistics' *Postcensal Estimates of the Resident Population of the United States for July 1, 2010–July 1, 2011, by Year, County, Single-Year of Age (0, 1, 2, . . ., 85 Years and Over), Bridged Race, Hispanic Origin, and Sex (Vintage 2011)* [machine-readable data files available online at www.cdc.gov/nchs/nvss/bridged_race.htm, as of 7/18/12].

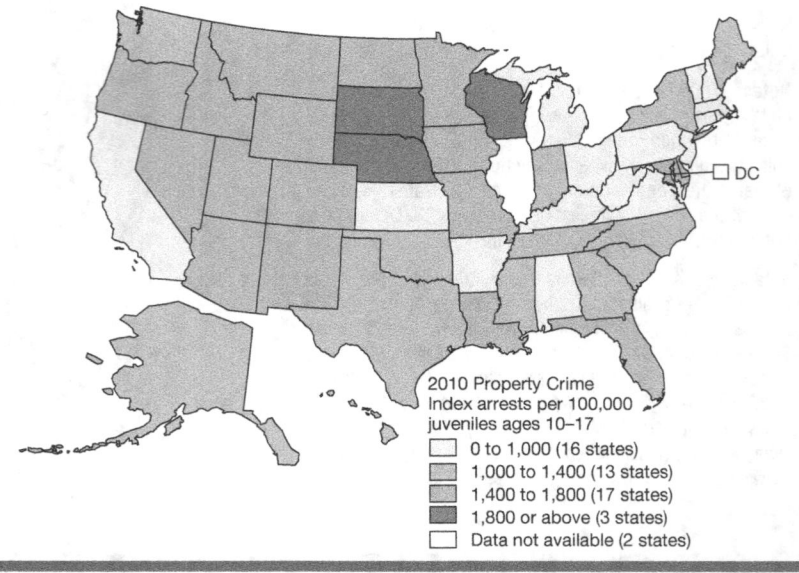

2010 Property Crime Index arrests per 100,000 juveniles ages 10–17
- ☐ 0 to 1,000 (16 states)
- 1,000 to 1,400 (13 states)
- 1,400 to 1,800 (17 states)
- 1,800 or above (3 states)
- ☐ Data not available (2 states)

# Notes

## Technical note

Although juvenile arrest rates may largely reflect juvenile behavior, many other factors can affect the magnitude of these rates. Arrest rates are calculated by dividing the number of youth arrests made in the year by the number of youth living in the jurisdiction. Therefore, jurisdictions that arrest a relatively large number of nonresident juveniles would have a higher arrest rate than jurisdictions where resident youth behave similarly. Jurisdictions (especially small ones) that are vacation destinations or that are centers for economic activity in a region may have arrest rates that reflect the behavior of nonresident youth more than that of resident youth.

Other factors that influence arrest rates in a given area include the attitudes of citizens toward crime, the policies of local law enforcement agencies, and the policies of other components of the justice system. In many areas, not all law enforcement agencies report their arrest data to the FBI. Rates for such areas are necessarily based on partial information and may not be accurate.

Comparisons of juvenile arrest rates across jurisdictions can be informative. Because of factors noted, however, comparisons should be made with caution.

## Arrest rate data source

Analysis of arrest data from Snyder, H., and Mulako-Wantota, J., Bureau of Justice Statistics, *Arrest Data Analysis Tool* [available online at www.bjs.gov/index. cfm?ty=datool&surl=/arrests/index.cfm, retrieved 11/8/12]; population data for 1980–1989 from the U.S. Census Bureau, *U.S. Population Estimates by Age, Sex, Race, and Hispanic Origin: 1980 to 1999* [machine-readable data files available online, released 4/11/00]; population data

for 1990–1999 from the National Center for Health Statistics (prepared by the U.S. Census Bureau with support from the National Cancer Institute), *Bridged-Race Intercensal Estimates of the July 1, 1990– July 1, 1999, United States Resident Population by County, Single-Year of Age, Sex, Race, and Hispanic Origin* [machine-readable data files available online at www.cdc.gov/nchs/nvss/bridged_race. htm, released 7/26/04]; population data for 2000–2009 from the National Center for Health Statistics (prepared under a collaborative arrangement with the U.S. Census Bureau), *Intercensal Estimates of the Resident Population of the United States for July 1, 2000–July 1, 2009, by Year, County, Single-Year of Age (0, 1, 2, . . ., 85 Years and Over), Bridged Race, Hispanic Origin, and Sex* [machine-readable data files available online at www.cdc.gov/nchs/nvss/bridged_race. htm, as of 10/26/12, following release by the U.S. Census Bureau of the revised unbridged intercensal estimates by 5-year age group on 10/9/12]; and population data for 2010 from the National Center for Health Statistics (prepared under a collaborative arrangement with the U.S. Census Bureau), *Postcensal Estimates of the Resident Population of the United States for July 1, 2010–July 1, 2011, by Year, County, Single-Year of Age (0, 1, 2, . . ., 85 Years and Over), Bridged Race, Hispanic Origin, and Sex (Vintage 2011)* [machine-readable data files available online at www.cdc.gov/ nchs/nvss/bridged_race.htm, as of 7/18/12, following release by the U.S. Census Bureau of the unbridged vintage 2011 postcensal estimates by 5-year age group on 5/17/12].

## Data coverage

FBI arrest data in this bulletin are counts of arrests detailed by age of arrestee and offense categories from all law enforcement agencies that reported complete

data for the calendar year. (See *Crime in the United States 2010* for offense definitions.) The proportion of the U.S. population covered by these reporting agencies ranged from 63% to 94% between 1980 and 2010, with 2010 coverage of 81%.

Estimates of the number of persons in each age group in the reporting agencies' resident populations assume that the resident population age profiles are like the nation's. Reporting agencies' total populations were multiplied by the U.S. Census Bureau's most current estimate of the proportion of the U.S. population for each age group.

The reporting coverage for the total United States (84%) in the tables on pages 21 and 22 includes all states reporting arrests of persons younger than age 18. This is greater than the coverage in the rest of the bulletin (81%) for various reasons. For example, a state may provide arrest counts of persons younger than age 18 but not provide the age detail required to support other subpopulation estimates.

---

**Visit OJJDP's Statistical Briefing Book for more information on juvenile arrests**

OJJDP's online Statistical Briefing Book (SBB) offers access to a wealth of information about juvenile crime and victimization and about youth involved in the juvenile justice system. Visit the "Law Enforcement and Juvenile Crime" section of the SBB at ojjdp.gov/ojstatbb/crime/faqs.asp for more information about juvenile arrest rate trends detailed by offense, gender, and race, including a spreadsheet of all juvenile arrest rates used in this bulletin.

---

www.ingramcontent.com/pod-product-compliance
Lightning Source LLC
Chambersburg PA
CBHW081144280526
45787CB00007B/3218